Published in 2020
First published in the UK by Igloo Books Ltd
An imprint of Igloo Books Ltd
Cottage Farm, NN6 0BJ, UK
Owned by Bonnier Books
Sveavägen 56, Stockholm, Sweden
www.igloobooks.com

1120 001
2 4 6 8 10 9 7 5 3 1
ISBN 978-1-80022-442-1

Cover Images: tc Science History Images / Alamy Stock Photo;
bl United Archives GmbH / Alamy Stock Photo;
bc Niday Picture Library / Alamy Stock Photo
All other images: © iStock / Getty Images

Designed by Jess Brown
Edited by Bobby Newlyn-Jones
Written by Will Bryan

Printed and manufactured in China

CONSPIRACY THEORIES

A FASCINATING AND INSIGHTFUL LOOK AT THE WORLD'S BIGGEST MYSTERIES

CONTENTS

THE TRUTH IS OUT THERE

Often history is written or told by people who want to keep some things hidden and truth is the casualty. Conspiracy theorists, aware that not all the information has been revealed, tend to see secret plots behind the world's great events. They see the world in terms of megalomaniac secret societies, controlling regimes, criminal gangs, terrorists and aliens.

Sometimes these theories seem far-fetched or paranoid, but sometimes they reveal something hidden, and sometimes, just sometimes, they uncover a truth which is, quite literally, beyond belief.

History has been distorted and manipulated, glossed over, or quite simply ignored. At other points, false information has been fed to us—fake news is nothing new. Hoaxes litter the landscape, giving rise to legends and false beliefs, and giving others the opportunity to dismiss the truth. The Piltdown Man, for years reckoned to be the infamous missing link between humans and apes, later turned out to be a hoax. Some believed fairies to be real for a long time, and the likes of Bigfoot, the Loch Ness Monster and even the Turin Shroud are still disputed.

Is the world as we know it a hoax on a larger scale?

The truth isn't all about lies, either, but is sometimes veiled by mystery and is very much out there to be found. True identities, for example, like those of Jack the Ripper and Shakespeare, have gripped speculators for centuries. Disappearances like those of Lord Lucan and Amelia Earhart are still speculated over. Questions continue across a multitude of subjects.

There's more, so much more, and this book will help you to scratch the surface.

POLITICAL ASSASSINATIONS

Who killed them and why? The deaths of well-known people continue to be discussed often long after their lives and achievements have started to fade into history.

Many people who know little of President Abraham Lincoln's politics know that he was shot while watching a play. Many people alive in 1963 remember where they were the day JFK was shot and many others share in the conspiracy theories about who fired or inspired that fateful shot. The deaths of Robert Kennedy and Martin Luther King, murdered in 1968, also cause comment and controversy to this day. Websites teem with views on how and when the U.S. tried to get rid of Cuba's Fidel Castro and whether or not Hitler actually killed himself. Fact and fiction become interleaved, whodunit theories proliferate and the conspiracy behind the assassin's bullet becomes more impenetrable still, darker than the deed itself.

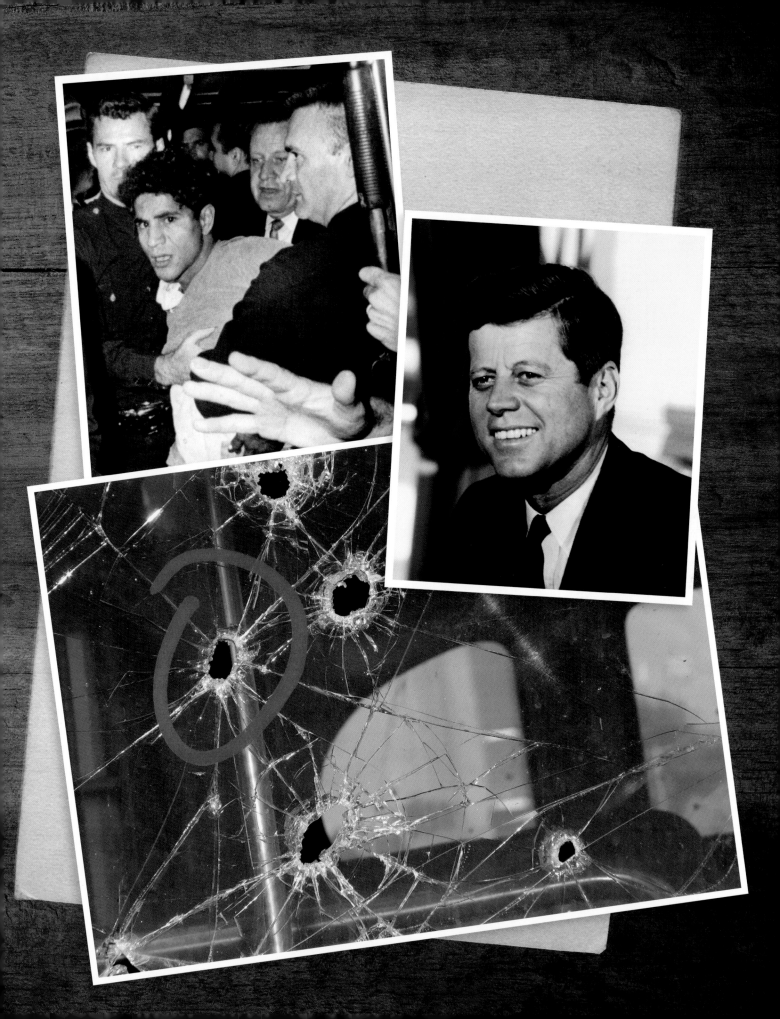

WHO SHOT JFK?

Who shot President Kennedy? His shooting in Dallas has kept conspiracy theorists busy ever since that fateful day in 1963.

President John F. Kennedy died at 1:00 pm on November 22, 1963, in Parkland Hospital, Dallas. At 12:30 pm, the president and Mrs Kennedy had been in a motorcade passing the Texas School Book Depository. Kennedy waved to the crowd. Three shots rang out. The first missed, the second passed through the president's neck and hit Texas Governor John Connally. The third struck Kennedy in the head, fatally. At 1:15 pm, Dallas policeman JD Tippit was shot dead trying to stop and question a man. The killer ran into a cinema, where he was arrested. He was Lee Harvey Oswald.

What was the evidence against Oswald? Policeman Marrion Baker saw Oswald leaving the Book Depository building, where a rifle was found. Oswald had rifle training in the U.S. Marines, but some experts doubted he was a crack marksman. Conspiracy theorists question whether Oswald could have fired three shots in less than eight seconds. Oswald had spent time in the Soviet Union and had a Russian wife. So was he a pro-Communist fanatic, or had he been set up by a bigger conspiracy to get rid of Kennedy? Did Oswald act alone? Or was there a second shooter?

Oswald was charged with double murder (Kennedy and Tippit), but never reached a courtroom. On November 24, while he was being moved to the county jail, nightclub owner Jack Ruby pushed through reporters and shot him. Oswald died soon afterward. This sparked more questions. How had the Dallas police let Ruby get so close with a .38 gun, yelling "You killed the President, you rat!" Was Ruby part of the conspiracy? He died in 1967, from cancer, leaving the mystery unsolved.

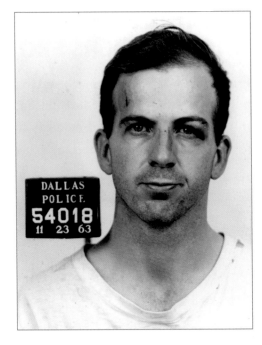

Above: Lee Harvey Oswald tried to kill Major General Edwin A. Walker on April 10, 1963. His garbled writings revealed a man with a grudge against the U.S. political establishment.

Left: President and Mrs Kennedy rode through Dallas in a motorcade. In the front seat of the presidential car was Texas state governor John Connally, wounded in the shooting.

EVIDENCE?

OSWALD BOUGHT A RIFLE BY MAIL ORDER AND IT'S ALLEGED THIS WAS THE WEAPON RECOVERED FROM THE SCHOOL BOOK DEPOSITORY. HE USED A REVOLVER TO KILL OFFICER TIPPIT. LATER, IT WAS SUGGESTED THAT OSWALD HAD DEFECTED TO THE SOVIET UNION AND THE REAL ASSASSIN WAS A RUSSIAN AGENT. IT WAS ARGUED THAT THE U.S. GOVERNMENT SUPPRESSED THE FACT TO AVOID A THIRD WORLD WAR. THE BODY WAS EXHUMED IN 1981, BUT WAS DECLARED TO BE THAT OF LEE HARVEY OSWALD.

JFK FILES RELEASED IN 2017, UNDER ORDERS FROM TRUMP

President Donald Trump promised to release all the U.S. government's files on JFK and, at least partially, he delivered on this. In the event, 28,000 previously classified files were released to the public. These included some revelations, including:

- Lee Harvey Oswald spoke to a member of the KGB assassination unit (Department 13), at the Soviet embassy on September 28, 1963, and called the embassy on October 1, speaking in Russian.

- The FBI warned Dallas police of a threat to kill Oswald after his arrest, according to a memo by J. Edgar Hoover, who was head of the FBI at the time.

- FBI officers were looking for Oswald before the assassination, according to memos of the New Orleans division of the bureau.

- A British local newspaper was "warned in advance" of the assassination. An anonymous caller called the Cambridge Evening News, telling a reporter to call the U.S. embassy for some "big news," 25 minutes ahead of the shooting.

- The USSR was concerned that the U.S. could launch a missile strike. Soviet leaders, according to an FBI report, feared irresponsible action by generals in the absence of leadership at the top. They also considered Oswald a "neurotic maniac" who was possibly part of a right-wing conspiracy.

Below: Mrs Kennedy and other members of the President's family attend his funeral, November 25, 1963. His brother Bobby would also be assassinated less than five years later.

Above: JFK was buried at Arlington National Cemetery in Virginia. This famous cemetery has been the resting place for military personnel and their families dating back to the Civil War. Jacqueline Kennedy Onassis was buried nearby following her death in 1994.

Experts pored over the evidence, including cine-film taken by onlooker Abraham Zapruder. There were stories of a second gunman on a grassy knoll, who fled on a motorcycle. A myriad theories and allegations were aired about who wanted Kennedy dead—political rivals, anti-Catholics, Cubans, Russians, the Mafia, union bosses. Websites, books and films still explore the events of that day, many casting doubt on the official verdict. One theory aired in a book and on TV centered on one of the motorcade Secret Service agents, who (it was claimed) shot Kennedy by accident from the following car. A policeman claimed it was this agent's first time in the follow car, with an unfamiliar weapon, which went off either when the car stopped suddenly or in reaction to the first shot. The allegation, supposedly covered up by the government, on the orders of Johnson and Robert Kennedy, was strongly denied and contested by the agent (now dead). All that is clear is that after 1963 public life was never the same for any U.S. political leader.

THE TRUTH?

In 1964, U.S. Chief Justice Earl Warren's Commission concluded that Oswald had acted alone. In 1978, a committee of the House of Representatives accepted evidence that shots came from two locations and that Kennedy "was probably assassinated as a result of a conspiracy." In 1982 the U.S. National Research Council disagreed, but by then the conspiracy "suspects" in the frame included Lyndon Johnson, FBI boss J. Edgar Hoover, the Mafia, Cuban exiles (or Castro), the Soviet KGB, right-wing Republicans and fanatical anti-Catholics.

Right: At 11:21 pm Dallas time, Jack Ruby shoots the handcuffed Oswald, having walked into the garage from the Western Union office while the jail entrance was unguarded.

THE DEATH OF ABRAHAM LINCOLN

Abraham Lincoln, 16th president of the United States, was shot at a Washington theatre on April 15, 1865. He was the first U.S. president to be assassinated.

Lincoln is today lauded as one America's greatest presidents, but his presidency was dominated by the Civil War (1861–65). This bloody conflict almost broke the Union and created lasting bitterness. Lincoln, a hero to the anti-slavery movement, was hated and demonized by his enemies. By the spring of 1865, the strains of leadership were clear to see. In a rare moment of relaxation, he sat down to watch a play at Ford's Theatre in Washington.

Shortly after 10:00 pm, John Wilkes Booth, an actor of some repute but erratic temperament, entered the presidential box and shot Lincoln in the head. Attempting to leap on to the stage, the assassin fell, breaking his leg. Waving a dagger and uttering Virginia's state motto "Sic semper tyrannis" ("Always thus to tyrants"), Booth made his getaway.

Lincoln was taken to a house nearby, but died at 7:22 the next morning. Booth was tracked to a barn in Virginia and killed by Federal soldiers. His companion David Herold surrendered and talked. Booth's accomplices were rounded up: Mary Surratt, in whose home the plot had been hatched; David Herold; George Atzerodt, a carriage-builder; and Lewis Paine, an ex-soldier. They were found guilty by a military court of conspiring to kill Lincoln, vice president Andrew Johnson and secretary of state William H. Seward, and all four were hanged on July 7, 1865. Samuel Arnold and Michael O'Laughlin, friends of Booth, were found guilty of helping the conspiracy and given life sentences. So too was Samuel A. Mudd, the physician who had set Booth's broken leg. Edward Spangler, a stage hand at Ford's, was jailed for six years for helping Booth escape.

Above: A contemporary and melodramatic print illustrating the shocking murder of President Lincoln by Booth. The actor-assassin entered the Presidential box and fired from point-blank range, in full view of Mrs Lincoln.

EVIDENCE?

JOHN WILKES BOOTH WAS THE YOUNGER BROTHER OF THE GREAT ACTOR, EDWIN THOMAS BOOTH (1833–1893). BOOTH'S FIRST IDEA WAS TO KIDNAP LINCOLN AND HOLD HIM HOSTAGE FOR THE RELEASE OF CONFEDERATE PRISONERS. HE SEEMS TO HAVE DECIDED TO KILL THE PRESIDENT WHEN NEWS CAME OF ROBERT E. LEE'S SURRENDER TO ULYSSES S. GRANT ON APRIL 9, 1865. THE SOUTH WAS BEATEN AND LEE HAD EFFECTIVELY ENDED THE WAR. BOOTH SHOT LINCOLN FIVE DAYS LATER.

Right: A wanted poster issued by the police hunting down Booth and two of his co-conspirators, John Surratt and David Herold (here misspelled as Harold). The reward offered was huge. In 2020, the equivalent value would be more than $1.5 million.

SURRAT.   BOOTH.   HAROLD.

War Department, Washington, April 20, 1865,

$100,000 REWARD!

THE MURDERER

Of our late beloved President, Abraham Lincoln,

IS STILL AT LARGE.

$50,000 REWARD

Will be paid by this Department for his apprehension, in addition to any reward offered by Municipal Authorities or State Executives.

$25,000 REWARD

Will be paid for the apprehension of JOHN H. SURRATT, one of Booth's Accomplices.

$25,000 REWARD

Will be paid for the apprehension of David C. Harold, another of Booth's accomplices.

LIBERAL REWARDS will be paid for any information that shall conduce to the arrest of either of the above-named criminals, or their accomplices.

All persons harboring or secreting the said persons, or either of them, or aiding or assisting their concealment or escape, will be treated as accomplices in the murder of the President and the attempted assassination of the Secretary of State, and shall be subject to trial before a Military Commission and the punishment of DEATH.

Let the stain of innocent blood be removed from the land by the arrest and punishment of the murderers. All good citizens are exhorted to aid public justice on this occasion. Every man should consider his own conscience charged with this solemn duty, and rest neither night nor day until it be accomplished.

EDWIN M. STANTON, Secretary of War.

DESCRIPTIONS.— BOOTH is Five Feet 7 or 8 inches high, slender build, high forehead, black hair, black eyes, and wears a heavy black moustache.

JOHN H. SURRAT is about 5 feet, 9 inches. Hair rather thin and dark; eyes rather light; no beard. Would weigh 145 or 150 pounds. Complexion rather pale and clear, with color in his cheeks. Wore light clothes of fine

Above: The single-shot Derringer pistol used to kill Lincoln. Easily concealed but powerful (.44 caliber), the gun is displayed at Ford's Theatre Museum in Washington, DC.

KILLING CASTRO

Cuba's Fidel Castro was a bogeyman to the U.S. government, after his 1959 revolution brought Communism to within a boat-ride of the United States mainland.

Cuban exiles pressed for direct action against Castro, and in 1961 President Kennedy approved the disastrous Bay of Pigs landing by exiles, backed by the CIA but without full-scale military support. The disgruntled CIA considered various schemes to get rid of Castro, such as Operation 40, which involved sabotage and Operation Northwoods, a "false flag" conspiracy. Northwoods' plotters allegedly schemed to stage terrorist acts, such as plane hijacks and urban bombings, in the United States. They would then pin the blame on Castro and so give the U.S. an excuse to launch a strike on Cuba. The Northwoods planners even considered sabotaging the spaceflight by Mercury astronaut John Glenn. After CIA director Allen W. Dulles was forced to quit in 1961, President Kennedy rejected Northwoods outright.

The CIA, however, continued to plot how to neutralize, politically ruin or eliminate Castro. The "kill Castro" scenarios included using a mistress to give Castro poison pills in bed; injecting Castro "accidentally" with a poisoned pen; slipping him an exploding cigar to blow off his head; and secretly lacing his meals with chemicals to make his hair and beard fall out, thus destroying his macho revolutionary image.

Knowing Castro's fondness for scuba diving, the CIA considered offering him a contaminated wetsuit as a diplomatic gift. Wearing the toxic suit would give him a fatal disease. Another plot involved planting alluring but explosive-packed conch shells on the sea bed for Castro to pick up for his shell collection.

Castro remained an irritant to the U.S. government, until, forced into retirement in 2008 by ill-health, he handed power to his younger brother Raul.

Above: Fidel Castro in the 1960s. By then the Cuban leader had become the USA's diplomatic enemy number 1.

EVIDENCE?

THE "CUBAN PROJECT" CAMPAIGN BY THE CIA TO OVERTHROW THE COMMUNIST REGIME IN CUBA WAS OFTEN PURSUED WITHOUT THE KNOWLEDGE OF THE U.S. PRESIDENT. AT ITS PEAK, SOME 2,500 PEOPLE WERE EMPLOYED IN ANTI-CASTRO PLOTS! CRITICS LAMBASTED THE CIA FOR ABSURD AND COSTLY FAILURE, MAKING THE UNITED STATES APPEAR "THE WORLD'S BIGGEST TERRORIST."

Left: A missile-laden Soviet freighter is escorted out of Cuban waters by a U.S. Navy plane and destroyer in October 1962. This is the end of the Cuban Missile Crisis.

Above: Castro, in conference
with his revolutionary lieutenant
Ernesto "Che" Guevara.

Above: A memorial outside The Bay of Pigs
Museum in Cuba, dedicated to all those who were
killed in the 1961 landing.

ROBERT KENNEDY KILLED

The world was shocked in 1968 by the killing of Robert (Bobby) Kennedy, brother of the murdered president, John F. Kennedy. Was the killer a lone gunman, as charged, or was Kennedy another conspiracy victim?

Conspiracy theorists dispute the verdict that the killer was Sirhan Sirhan alone and look for evidence of a conspiracy by people with a grudge against Bobby Kennedy. He had made enemies as a campaigning lawyer investigating links between organized crime and corrupt union bosses, and as a civil rights supporter. In 1960, he helped John Kennedy win the presidential election. He then served as Attorney General, first to President Kennedy and then to President Johnson. Many Americans saw "RFK" as the natural heir to "JFK." In 1968, the Kennedy bandwagon was rolling. Senator Kennedy was well placed to secure the Democratic nomination for president and succeed Lyndon Johnson—and then he was shot. Sirhan claimed to have no memory of his actions, but also said he'd killed Kennedy because Bobby supported Israel. Conspiracy theorists allege a second gunman, possibly a girl in a polka-dot dress seen running away. Controversy focused on the fatal shots. Audio recordings suggested more shots were fired than the eight Sirhan's gun held. Sirhan's "amnesia," it was claimed, was the result of mind-control, maybe by CIA or Mafia controllers.

Above: Bobby Kennedy attending a meeting at the White House in 1964, during his time as Attorney General.

Below: The Ambassador Hotel, Los Angeles, where Kennedy was killed. Famed for the Coconut Grove nightclub, the hotel was demolished in 2005.

Right: Sirhan Sirhan was apprehended at the scene of the murder.

Below: Bobby Kennedy lies stricken on the floor of the Ambassador Hotel in Los Angeles after being shot at close range.

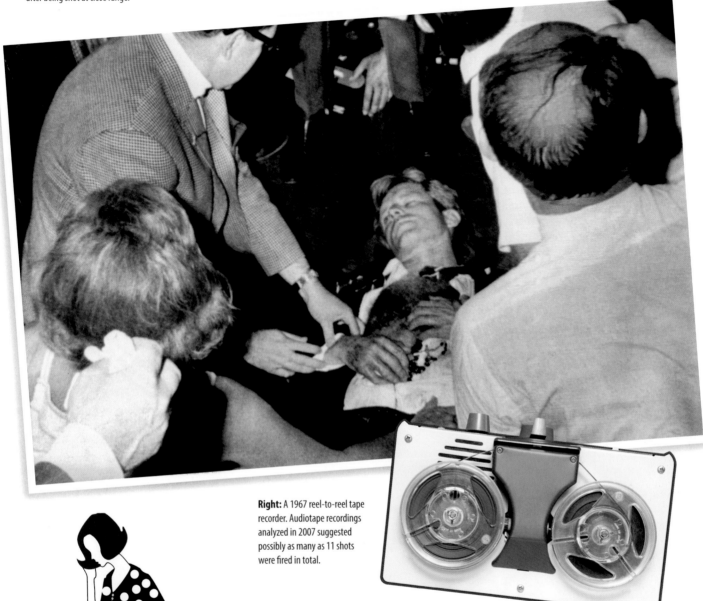

Right: A 1967 reel-to-reel tape recorder. Audiotape recordings analyzed in 2007 suggested possibly as many as 11 shots were fired in total.

Left: A mystery girl in a polka-dot dress was alleged to have left the murder scene with a companion, shouting "we shot him!" A second shooter fits in with gunshot evidence, according to some theorists.

AT A GLANCE

BOBBY KENNEDY WAS SHOT AT CLOSE RANGE WHILE WALKING THROUGH A CROWDED KITCHEN PASSAGE IN THE AMBASSADOR HOTEL, LOS ANGELES. HE DIED 26 HOURS LATER. PALESTINIAN IMMIGRANT SIRHAN SIRHAN, AGE 24, FIRED THE SHOTS FROM A .22 GUN, HARDLY THE WEAPON OF CHOICE FOR A PRO HITMAN. HE WAS ARRESTED ON THE SPOT, BUT HIS DEATH SENTENCE WAS LATER COMMUTED TO LIFE IN JAIL.

Above: The mugshot of James Earl Ray. He fled the country after the assassination, but was caught at London's Heathrow Airport. He pleaded guilty and received a 99-year prison term. In 1977, Ray escaped from jail for three days. He died in prison in 1998, aged 70.

WHO KILLED KING?

US civil rights activist Martin Luther King was shot dead on April 4, 1968. King had enemies, but many more friends who admired his achievements. So who assassinated this man of peace?

Was King the victim of a conspiracy? Some of those closest to him believed so, and in 1999 a civil trial reaffirmed this view. Jesse Jackson, civil rights leader and a colleague of King, was quoted in 2004 alleging there were "saboteurs" within the civil rights movement. Jackson could not accept that King's killer was escaped convict James Earl Ray. King had been the frequent target of racist attacks, including the bombing of his home. In April 1968, King was in Memphis, Tennessee, to support striking garbage workers. He was shot while standing on his motel balcony. The Civil Rights Act of 1968 marked a major step toward the equality for which he had striven.

Below: Investigators on the balcony of Room 306 of the Lorraine Motel in Memphis, Tennessee, where Reverend Martin Luther King was shot dead on April 4, 1968.

20

Below: Famed for his 1963 "I have a dream" speech, Nobel Laureate Martin Luther King was America's most high-profile civil rights leader and an eloquent spokesman for African-Americans and the underprivileged. This high profile made him a target.

Above: The Poor People's March in Washington, DC— a campaign begun by King in 1968. His support for such movements and his opposition to the Vietnam War, are possible reasons that power-brokers wanted him removed.

AT A GLANCE

KING'S DEATH PROVOKED GRIEF, RAGE AND RIOTS ACROSS AMERICA. PUBLIC FIGURES OFTEN ATTRACT THE INTEREST —SOMETIMES MURDEROUS—OF LONERS AND ATTENTION-SEEKERS. BUT WAS RAY SUCH A MAN? IN 1978, A U.S. CONGRESS COMMITTEE SUGGESTED THERE WAS A "LIKELIHOOD" THAT RAY DID NOT ACT ALONE IN KILLING DR KING. RAY HIMSELF, KNOWN TO HAVE RACIST VIEWS, CLAIMED A MAN NAMED RAUL HAD BEEN INVOLVED AND BLAMED THE U.S. GOVERNMENT. BALLISTIC TESTS PROVED INCONCLUSIVE.

HITLER SUICIDE?

Did Adolf Hitler, the Nazi leader who had plunged the world into war, really die in April 1945 as the Soviet armies closed in? Did he kill himself, as the official histories claim? Or did Hitler escape and live on?

Right: Adolf Hitler (in 1937). One bizarre theory claims Hitler had himself cloned. More credible is the suggestion that he had his lookalike "doppelganger," Gustav Weler, shot in an attempt to confuse the Allied troops, while he himself escaped from Berlin.

On April 28, 1945, as Soviet guns and tanks pounded Berlin, Adolf Hitler married Eva Braun in the Führer's underground bunker. The Nazi leader vowed he would not be taken prisoner. In the early hours of April 29, Hitler dictated for the last time to his secretary, Traudl Junge. Later, doubting the cyanide capsules he had been given, he ordered that they be tested on his dog, Blondi. To his distress, the dog died. On April 30, Hitler retired at 3:00 pm to his sitting room with Eva. At about 3:15 pm a shot was fired. Hitler's valet, Heinz Linge, testified he found Hitler dead, shot in the head. Hitler and Eva had also taken cyanide.

The bodies were wrapped in a rug, doused in petrol and burned in a shell-crater. The survivors fled, to be killed, captured, or to disappear. On May 4, Soviet soldiers found charred remains of humans and two dogs, but Soviet leader Josef Stalin told American diplomats he believed Hitler had escaped.

Below: The suggested "escape route" to South America involved a flight from Berlin, followed by an ocean-crossing in a U-boat. Two German U-boats arrived in Argentina in the summer of 1945.

ESCAPE ROUTE

1 Berlin, Germany

2 Tonder, Denmark

3 Travemunde, Germany

4 Reus, Spain

5 Fuerteventura, Canary Isles

6 Mar Del Plata, Argentina

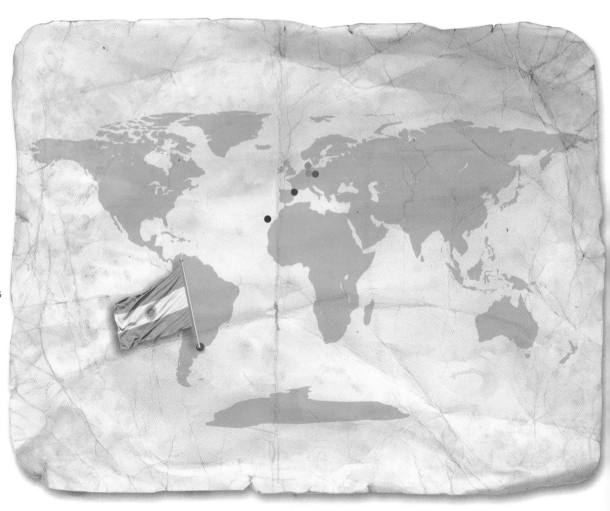

THE STARS AND STRIPES

PARIS EDITION

Daily Newspaper of U.S. Armed Forces in the European Theater of Operations

EXTRA   EXTRA

Vol. 1—No. 279   Wednesday, May 2, 1945   1 Fr.

HITLER DEAD

Fuehrer Fell at CP, German Radio Says; Doenitz at Helm, Vows War Will Continue

German radio announced last night that Adolf Hitler had died. Adm. Karl Doenitz, former commander-in-chief of the German Navy, has succeeded him as ruler of the Reich, the radio announcement said.

Doenitz made a radio speech immediately after the announcement, Reuter said, and declared that Germany would continue to wage war. His statement spiked peace rumors which had been prevalent for more than a week in all world capitals.

Churchill Hints Peace Is at Hand

Winston Churchill indicated to a brief address to Commons yesterday that peace in Europe might come before Saturday.

Pope Prepares Speech

Top and above: Dr Josef Mengele, the Auschwitz "Angel of Death", fled to South America—as did Adolf Eichmann. Mengele was never caught, but Eichmann was found, tried and executed in Israel.

Left and above: On May 2, 1945, Allied soldiers read news of Hitler's death in the U.S. Army newspaper; the gun he used was reputedly a Walther PPK such as this one.

Stories circulated of a secret tunnel, through which Hitler had fled. The official Soviet Communist line was that Hitler could have fled to Spain, Argentina or even Japan. Later theories were wildly fantastic, suggesting, for example, that Hitler had escaped to a South Pole Nazi hideout that concealed an "inner world" (the Earth was hollow). The most bizarre theory was that Hitler flew, in a space rocket version of the V-2 missile, to a secret Moon base.

THE TRUTH?

Conspiracy theories suggest that Hitler faked his death and escaped to Argentina, where he lived with Eva until his death in 1962. Russian officials insist that a fragment of skull with a bullet hole in it, kept in the Russian State Archive, is proof of Hitler's suicide. However, American scientists disagree. After performing DNA tests on the skull in 2009, they claim it came from a woman aged under 40, not a man aged 56.

SPIES AND WAR

Silent conspiracies are as much a part of warfare as battles and can be as deadly as the gun or bomb. Such has been the case ever since the Ancient Greeks tricked their way into Troy inside the wooden horse. And that secret insider information always has to come from somewhere.

Did the U.S. know of the Japanese plan to attack Pearl Harbor? Why were the code-breaking secrets of Bletchley Park concealed for so many years? The first casualty of war is truth, as fact and fiction become confused. Historians argue over what really happened, while conspiracy theorists offer alternative readings of events—stories that make fascinating, if not always credible, reading. During times of tension, such as the Cold War years of the 1940s to 1980s, the credible and incredible blur to become equally believable. Although what goes on behind closed doors is often only known by a few, it can be whispered about by millions and entrance a public ever more fascinated by a James Bond world of spies, moles, and secret military operations.

MOLES AND MURDERS

British prime minister Harold Wilson believed he was a target for the intelligence services. And was tycoon Robert Maxwell murdered by Israeli secret agents?

By the 1950s, most left-leaning politicians were anxious to shy away from any youthful flings with communism, in the hard light of Stalinist tyranny and Iron Curtain repression that had tarnished the socialist Utopian ideal. In the United States, McCarthyism had led to a vilification and witch-hunts for "reds under the bed."

Could it be that Labour leader Harold Wilson, Oxford don and Huddersfield Town football fan, was a Soviet mole? Soviet defector and ex-KGB man Anatoliy Golitsyn said he was, after hearing gossip in KGB corridors about secret poisons. According to Golitsyn, the KGB wanted to remove Hugh Gaitskell as Labour leader and install "their man" Wilson. Gaitskell died suddenly in 1963: the conspiracy version is that his fatal illness came after drinking poisoned coffee at the Soviet embassy. Wilson succeeded him, becoming Britain's prime minister in 1964. In his second term of office (1974–1976), Wilson apparently thought the British intelligence services were plotting against him, believed the lavatory in 10 Downing Street was bugged and told future president George H. W. Bush (then head of the CIA) that he was being spied on. Wilson's resignation in 1976 came as a surprise, though prime ministers Callaghan and Thatcher found no evidence of any plot against him "by or within the security service."

Above: British Labour leader Hugh Gaitskell and Harold Wilson arriving at Downing Street for a meeting with then-prime minister Howard MacMillan during the 1962 Cuban Missile Crisis. By 1964, Gaitskell was dead and Wilson was prime minister.

Left: Harold Wilson in 1964. The Wilson government remained an ally of the United States, but refused to commit troops to the Vietnam War.

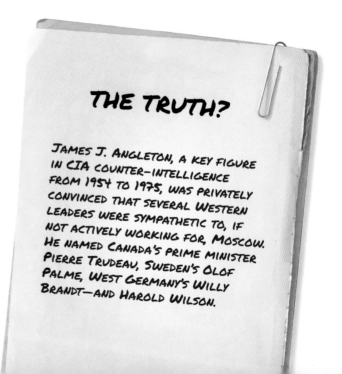

THE TRUTH?

James J. Angleton, a key figure in CIA counter-intelligence from 1954 to 1975, was privately convinced that several Western leaders were sympathetic to, if not actively working for, Moscow. He named Canada's prime minister Pierre Trudeau, Sweden's Olof Palme, West Germany's Willy Brandt—and Harold Wilson.

A prominent figure in the Wilson years and later was publishing boss Robert Maxwell. Born Jan Hoch in Czechoslovakia, Maxwell (it was alleged) became a Soviet agent during World War II, at the same time as he was winning medals in the British Army. In his post-war publishing career, Maxwell did many deals across the Iron Curtain and prospered. It has also been alleged that he was at the same time working for the Israeli secret service, Mossad. The story is that by 1990, with his empire in financial meltdown, Maxwell was asked by the KGB to help remove Russian reformer Mikhail Gorbachev in return for cash. He was supposed to bring the Israelis (and through them the Americans) on board, but the Israelis refused. Maxwell demanded a pay-off to solve his business problems and keep quiet and was eliminated as a dangerous liability.

Below and top right: Robert Maxwell, seldom out of the news, owned Mirror Group Newspapers at the time he gave this press conference in April 1991. His businesses were in trouble and his death later that year aroused much speculation. The tycoon's body was found in the sea, supposedly after he died while alone on the deck of his yacht, *Lady Ghislaine*.

Below: Georgi Markov's widow, Annabel, was a key witness at the inquest into his death.

LICENSED TO KILL

Although, as far as we know, 007-style intrigue is not that common in the real world of espionage and counter-intelligence, mysterious deaths do sometimes happen.

In September 1978, Bulgarian writer and anti-communist dissident Georgi Markov died in a London hospital. Three days earlier he had felt unwell at his desk at the BBC World Service, complaining of a "sting" on his thigh. He had, it transpired, been the victim of a hit by Bulgarian secret agents. On September 8, Markov had been waiting at a bus stop when he felt something jab the back of his leg. Looking round, he saw a man picking up an umbrella. The man jumped into a cab. Markov became ill, but treatment in hospital failed to save him and he died three days later. An autopsy revealed that he had been "shot" with a tiny pellet containing toxic ricin, which had been absorbed into his bloodstream. There was no antidote to ricin poisoning.

A similarly mysterious but more public death came in 2006. Alexander Litvinenko was a former KGB agent, who had sought political asylum in Britain. He accused the Russian Federal Protective Service (FPS) of terrorist atrocities as part of its plan to destabilize the "new Russia" and insert Vladimir Putin as leader. Litvinenko had put himself in the line of fire. On November 1, 2006, he was taken ill with a mysterious radiation sickness and died three weeks later in hospital.

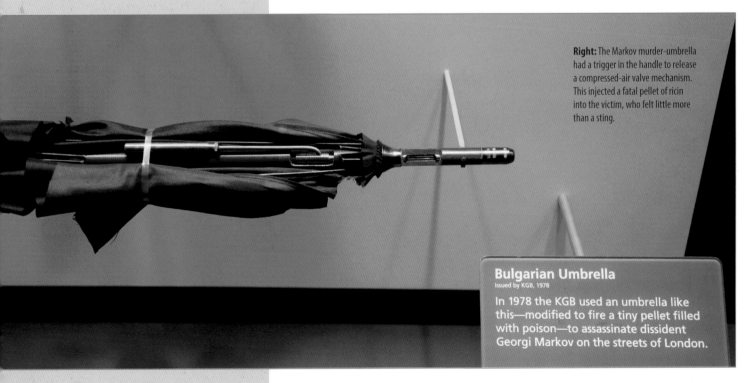

Right: The Markov murder-umbrella had a trigger in the handle to release a compressed-air valve mechanism. This injected a fatal pellet of ricin into the victim, who felt little more than a sting.

Bulgarian Umbrella
Issued by KGB, 1978

In 1978 the KGB used an umbrella like this—modified to fire a tiny pellet filled with poison—to assassinate dissident Georgi Markov on the streets of London.

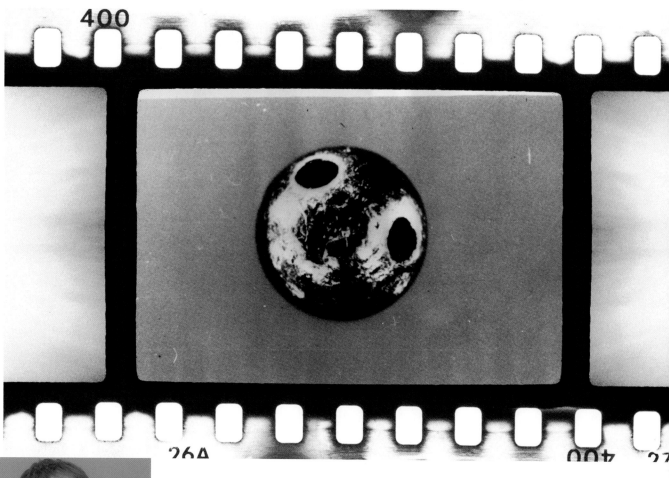

Above: A close up photograph of the tiny platinum pellet which killed Markov. The ball was filled with ricin, which was slowly released into his body.

Left: Andrei Lugovoi, suspected of involvement in the killing of Alexander Litvinenko, at a press conference in Moscow in 2007. Both Lugovoi and Litvinenko had links to the KGB.

Litvinenko had been poisoned with radioactive polonium-210, possibly at a sushi restaurant or in a cup of tea he drank at a London hotel. Russian agent Andrei Lugovoi was charged with murder in May 2007, provoking a furious diplomatic row between Britain and Russia, but by then he was back home out of reach. Later, a second Russian agent, Dmitri Kovtun, was also implicated. Neither is likely ever to be extradited to face trial, but in January 2015 a public inquiry finally began in London into Litvinenko's death.

THE TRUTH?

RADIATION POISON LEAVES A TRAIL. LITVINENKO'S ASSASSINS CONTAMINATED THEMSELVES WITH POLONIUM TRAVELING FROM GERMANY TO LONDON. TRACES WERE FOUND ON A COUCH IN A ROOM WHERE KOVTUN SPENT THE NIGHT, IN HIS CAR AND AT A RESTAURANT. LITVINENKO'S DEATHBED ACCUSATION THAT RUSSIAN INTELLIGENCE AND VLADIMIR PUTIN HAD CONSPIRED TO KILL HIM LED TO WORLDWIDE MEDIA COVERAGE. UNOFFICIALLY, THE BRITISH AUTHORITIES BELIEVED "WE ARE 100% SURE WHO ADMINISTERED THE POISON, WHERE AND HOW" BUT ANDREI LUGOVOI AND DMITRI KOVTUN WERE BY THEN THOUSANDS OF MILES AWAY.

THE CAMBRIDGE SPIES

In the 1950s, Britain's security services were made to look leaky. The Cambridge spies were revealed, only for three of them to escape across the Iron Curtain.

With the Cold War at its height, spies were all the rage in fiction. In reality too, "moles" and "sleepers" were deeply embedded in Britain's intelligence community. Most notorious were the "Cambridge spies", a group "converted" to communism and recruited as Soviet agents while students at Cambridge University in the 1930s. The four were Kim Philby, Guy Burgess, Donald Maclean and Anthony Blunt.

Of the four, the master spy was Philby. He joined MI6 in 1940 and later worked at the British embassy in Washington, acting as link between British intelligence and the Americans, while passing on secrets to the Russians at the height of the Cold War. Burgess and Maclean worked at the Foreign Office in London, also spying for the Russians. They got away with it until 1951, when both men disappeared, turning up publicly in Moscow in 1956. They had fled Britain after being tipped off by Philby, with whom Burgess had worked in Washington, that their cover as moles and spies was about to be blown. Philby maintained his cover, even after he was "named" as a double agent by a Labour MP in 1955, when he was "cleared" by the Foreign Office. However, he was shifted out of the diplomatic service and was working in the Lebanon as a journalist when, in 1963, he defected to the Soviet Union by sea, apparently fearing he was about to be abducted.

The Fourth Man was Sir Anthony Blunt, art expert and curator of the Queen's paintings. Blunt privately admitted to being a spy in 1964 in return for immunity from prosecution, but he was finally publicly unmasked in 1979 and stripped of his knighthood. How many secrets and how many Western agents were betrayed by the Cambridge spies is probably beyond estimation.

Above: Anthony Blunt had enjoyed a certain eminence as art adviser to the Queen, while secretly passing information to the Russians, a mission he had begun in the 1930s as a Cambridge recruiter of spies.

Top: Within the fairytale-looking Kremlin, the old Soviet leadership fought the Cold War—and conspired against one another.

Left: The headquarters of the Russian secret service in Moscow. During the Cold War, the KGB ran agents in many Western countries and between 1954 and 1991 was all-powerful.

Above: Kim Philby, most notorious of the so-called Cambridge spies. He defected to Russia in 1963.

THE TRUTH?

SPECULATION PERSISTED ABOUT A "FIFTH MAN." THERE WERE PROBABLY MORE THAN FIVE CAMBRIDGE SPIES. BLUNT (THE "TALENT-SPOTTER") AND BURGESS WERE MEMBERS OF THE APOSTLES, AN EXCLUSIVE UNIVERSITY SOCIETY. ANOTHER APOSTLE WAS JOHN CAIRNCROSS, NAMED AS A SOVIET SPY IN 1990. SOME HAVE CAST DOUBT ON THE DOUBLE ROLE OF SIR ROGER HOLLIS, MI5 BOSS FROM 1956 TO 1965.

SECRET WAR

World War II was a war of propaganda and secrets as much as military hardware. Secret agents crossed and double-crossed, and secret weapons were thought up and sketched on the backs of envelopes.

Britain had the better of things in the espionage war, with most German agents in the UK swiftly rounded up within months of the war starting in 1939. Some were jailed or executed, others "turned" into double-agents. It was never easy to tell who was who in the murky world of SIS and MI5, joined in 1940 by SOE, the Special Operations Executive, jokingly whispered of as "Churchill's Secret Army." Most spies were distinctly unglamorous—Arthur Owens, "a typical Welsh underfed type" according to his masters, ran a battery business, but was also agent SNOW working for the British and the Germans.

Backroom boffins devised all manner of weird ways in which to win the war. In 1944, German rocket scientists were frantically trying to turn defeat into victory with new super-weapons such as the V-2 rocket and the bat-winged Horten jet fighter.

Above: A German V-2 rocket, on display in Germany. Allied intelligence got wind of the secret super-weapon and knew there was no defense other than sabotage or bombing of rocket test sites and factories.

EVIDENCE

IN 1944, ALLIED PILOTS REPORTED SEEING BALLS OF FIRE ZIPPING AROUND AIRCRAFT. COULD THEY BE ENEMY SECRET WEAPONS? HALLUCINATIONS? UFOS? THE "FOO FIGHTERS" AS THEY WERE KNOWN (A TERM USED TO DESCRIBE ANY UNIDENTIFIED FLYING OBJECTS AT THE TIME) BECAME A WARTIME MYTH, FOR WHICH SCIENTISTS SUGGEST NATURAL PHENOMENA SUCH AS ST ELMO'S FIRE (BALL LIGHTNING) AS ONE EXPLANATION. A MORE FANCIFUL EXPLANATION WAS THAT THE GERMANS HAD INVENTED A FLYING SAUCER WITH WHIZZING GAS JETS (THE FIREBALL) TO DISRUPT ALLIED BOMBER FORMATIONS. HOWEVER, GERMAN AND JAPANESE PILOTS SAW "FOO FIGHTERS" TOO.

Above: A German radio operator of the Abwehr (Army intelligence). The German Army High Command ran reconnaissance (spying), signal-monitoring and counter-espionage operations.

German agents in France were being told to contaminate beer and wine, inject sausages with poison and prepare poisoned coffee, sugar, cigarettes and chocolate: the aim being to kill, disable and generally demoralize Allied soldiers and destabilize liberated areas.

The Allies dreamed up counter-schemes of doubtful utility. One idea was to bomb Berlin not with propaganda leaflets or high explosives, but with poisonous snakes! Another notion was to hit German food production by poisoning German cows with cabbage leaves dosed with toxins. As preparations were made for the 1944 Normandy landings, the British "miscellaneous weapons" department came up with a new idea for breaching the Nazis' much-vaunted Atlantic Wall. The Panjandrum was a rocket-propelled two-wheeled cart, packed with explosives. It was supposed to trundle out of the sea from a landing craft, roll up the beach, blast through concrete and steel defenses, and put the fear of God into the Germans. In trials, however, the Panjandrum showed an alarming tendency to run amok, spitting smoke and flames and sending its creators running in all directions. The eccentric project was quickly abandoned.

Right: *Careless Talk Costs Lives*: one of the war's most famous propaganda lines. Bomber pilots were ordered never to discuss missions, even with family, in case security was compromised. As it was, crews seldom knew targets in advance.

Keep mum
she's not so dumb!

CARELESS TALK COSTS LIVES

PEARL HARBOR

Right: Admiral Husband E. Kimmel, commanding the U.S. Pacific Fleet, bore the brunt of criticism for U.S. military failings at Pearl Harbor. He was relieved of his command.

The Japanese attack on Pearl Harbor, on December 7, 1941, brought the United States into World War II. Was it a surprise? Conspiracy theorists maintain that American (and British) intelligence knew of Japan's plan. The U.S. administration allowed Pearl Harbor to bring America into the war.

In 1941, the war in Europe was still going Germany's way. In Asia, Japan was winning in China and was planning imperial expansion in the Pacific. U.S. intelligence analyst Arthur H. McCollum suggested that only a direct attack on the U.S. would sway a war-shy American public, even though Britain's prime minister, Winston Churchill, was desperate for U.S. aid and was urging President Roosevelt to join the conflict. U.S. Secretary of War Henry Stimson was expecting "impending hostilities" and so was shocked when the U.S. Navy was caught unawares by the Japanese planes that roared in to devastate Pearl Harbor.

Did Churchill know what was coming, but keep quiet? Did secret telegrams from London warn of Japanese intentions? Some historians claim the British had cracked the JN-25 naval code and knew of Japan's plans. The Americans did not pick up radio traffic, since the Japanese battle fleet used only flags and light signals. General "war warnings" were given to U.S. forces, but nothing specific about Pearl. Why were the three U.S. carriers out of port? Was it a ploy, to keep them out of danger? And if so, why leave eight battleships at anchor?

THE TRUTH?

THE U.S. NAVY BELIEVED PEARL HARBOR WAS TOO SHALLOW FOR A TORPEDO ATTACK. LIAISON BETWEEN THE ARMY AND NAVY WAS POOR, RADAR RUDIMENTARY AND TRAINING LEISURELY. ALL THREE CARRIERS WERE AWAY, BUT USS ENTERPRISE MIGHT HAVE BEEN HIT HAD IT RETURNED ON TIME.

Right: The USS Arizona war memorial at Pearl Harbor, commemorating the 2,388 people killed in the Japanese attack.

TO THE MEMORY OF THE GALLANT MEN HERE ENTOMBED AND THEIR SHIPMATES WHO GAVE THEIR LIVES IN ACTION ON DECEMBER 7, 1941 ON THE U.S.S. ARIZONA

THIS MEMORIAL WALL WAS INSTALLED AND REDEDICATED BY AMVETS APRIL 4, 1984

Above: Sailors in a launch rescue a man from the water as the battleship *USS West Virginia* burns following the Japanese attack. Eight U.S. battleships were in Pearl Harbor.

Right: Posters demanding vengeance roused an angry American public, now ready for war not just in the Pacific but in Europe as well.

AVENGE December 7

CODEBREAKERS AND D-DAY

The D-Day landings in 1944 marked the beginning of the end of World War II in Europe. Behind the vast armada lay a hidden army of codebreakers and planners.

Hardly anyone knew the secrets of a Victorian mansion estate 80 km (50 miles) northwest of London. Bletchley Park, codenamed Station X, was home to a small army of codebreakers. Here almost every German secret signal was read and passed on by Station X's backroom geniuses, among them mathematicians Alan Turing and Max Newman and Post Office engineer Tommy Flowers, who together helped create Colossus, the world's first programmable computer.

Helped by the Poles, who got hold of an Enigma cipher machine, the British had cracked Germany's military codes by 1940. The Germans had put too much faith in Enigma and in the Lorenz cipher used by Hitler to communicate with his generals, but read by Station X, even though its codebreakers had never seen a Lorenz machine. The British shared their intelligence, codenamed Ultra, with the Americans.

Station X's codebreakers were crucial to the success of the Normandy landings on June 6, 1944. The Germans knew the invasion was coming, but not its location, and to mask the true battle plan—Allied deception strategists did their utmost to confuse the enemy.

Below: Two British naval Wrens adjust Colossus Mk II, the revolutionary programmable computer at Bletchley Park in England that greatly helped the success of D-Day. This computer had 2,500 vacuum tubes (valves).

Below: Bletchley Park, codename Station X, where the first codebreakers arrived under cover as a "shooting party" in September 1938.

Top left: Enigma was a 1918 banking design, modified in the 1930s by the German military so they could send coded messages. They put too much faith in its security.

They laid false trails everywhere, such as a nonexistent U.S. army "based" in eastern England, with dummy airfields and dummy planes. Fake documents planted on a dead "British officer" (later known as "The Man Who Never Was") suggested to the Germans that Calais, not Normandy, was the Allies' target. Meanwhile "Monty's double," a Montgomery look-alike, toured bases in the Mediterranean to suggest to the Germans that the British commander was planning an attack in southern France.

Commandos were landed secretly on beaches in France to test out the sand and tides. Yet no deception could conjure an unopposed landing, so among the orthodox preparations for battle on the beaches were some "hush-hush" invasion-machines. These ingenious weapons, known as "Hobart's Funnies" (after Major General Percy Hobart) included "swimming" DD tanks (Shermans with propellers), Crab tanks armed with flails to detonate land mines, the Crocodile flame-thrower and Bobbin tanks, which laid a canvas strip of roadway for transport following behind.

Below: Allied troops land on D-Day. To confuse the Germans, miniature dummy paratroops nicknamed "Ruperts" were also dropped from planes, complete with firecrackers to make them look more convincing.

Above: The Utah Beach D-Day Museum in Normandy.

THE TRUTH?

NORMANDY WAS CHOSEN AS THE D-DAY TARGET BECAUSE THE GERMANS DID NOT EXPECT AN ATTACK THERE—THE REGION LACKED PORTS FOR AN INVADING ARMY. SO THE ALLIES BUILT TWO PREFABRICATED HARBORS MADE FROM CONCRETE AND STEEL SECTIONS. KNOWN AS "MULBERRIES," THEY WERE TOWED BY 150 TUGS ACROSS THE CHANNEL. THEY SERVED THEIR PURPOSE, ALTHOUGH ONE WAS SOON WRECKED BY FIERCE CHANNEL STORMS.

GOVERNMENT COVER-UPS

Few things attract conspiracy theorists more than the idea that we are being lied to or deceived, especially when the deception is being made by those who are supposed to lead and protect us. What is it they don't want us to know, and why?

It may sound completely paranoid, but the truth is that there has been a historical precedent for those in charge to feed us half-truths or even complete lies. Sometimes these lies are exposed and those in charge are held to account, such as the Watergate scandal, but sometimes we are left scratching our heads by the inconsistencies and real-life plot holes left behind. An astounding possibility is that we might be being exposed to mind-controlling substances in vapor trails and water. Just as astounding is the suggestion that Neil Armstrong's historic first Moon-step in 1969 never happened, since the Apollo landing was a fake—a front for one of the most audacious cons of all time.

FLUORIDE IN THE WATER

Is adding fluoride to water a safe way to ensure gleaming white, cavity-free smiles? In 1969, the World Health Organization endorsed fluoridation. But was fluoride a dental breakthrough or a sinister side-effect of the atomic age infringing rights and threatening health?

Fluorides are compounds containing fluorine (chemical symbol F). In the 1930s, scientists discovered that fluoride reduces tooth decay. By the 1950s, many Americans were drinking fluoridated water and using fluoride toothpaste.

Critics cited harmful side-effects of fluoride, both to teeth and health in general. On ethical grounds they argued that fluoridation violated the Human Rights Act and the UN Convention on the Rights of the Child. Supporters retorted that fluoride posed minimal health risks, in return for fewer fillings. A healthy fluoride level in water of 1 part per million was considered "safe."

Conspiracy theorists take the view that fluoridation was part of a plan to control the American people. In 1945, U.S. scientist Charles Perkins was told by a German fluoride manufacturer that the Germans had added fluoride to water to keep prisoners docile.

Did government agencies take note? Recently declassified documents have revealed that vast quantities of toxic fluoride were needed to make the first atomic bombs and fluoride became a major health hazard to people working for the bomb program. It's alleged that "Program F" was a U.S. cover-up. Evidence of fluoride's dangers were suppressed and instead fluoride was promoted as a dental marvel. The debate continues.

Above: The Trinity atomic bomb test, July 1945. Fluoride use in the top-secret Manhattan A-bomb project is said to have caused environmental and health damage. Was the "fluoride is good for teeth" campaign a cover-up and Cold War paranoia an excuse to bury bad news?

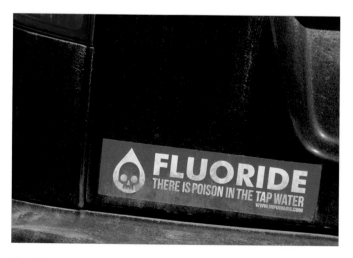

Above: Many people believe that fluoride is toxic, and are willing to express their views.

THE TRUTH?

IN ENGLAND, ABOUT 10% OF PEOPLE DRINK FLUORIDATED WATER. IN THE U.S. THE FIGURE IS ABOUT 60%. CANADA, AUSTRALIA, NEW ZEALAND AND IRELAND ALL FLUORIDATE WATER. EUROPE IS LESS KEEN: GERMANY, FRANCE, BELGIUM AND SWITZERLAND ALL DO NOT. COUNTRIES THAT DON'T FLUORIDATE WATER ALSO REPORT FALLS IN DENTAL DECAY; POSSIBLY BECAUSE OF FLUORIDE TOOTHPASTE, IMPROVING ORAL HYGIENE AND DIET.

Above: Fit to drink? Since the 1950s people have trusted water companies to supply clean water. This involves chemical treatment, but how much is ethical?

Above: An anti-fluoride protest was held in San Francisco in 2013. The "fluoride prevents tooth decay" myth is, skeptics claim, a smokescreen to hide health fears, even its use as a mind-control agent.

Above: Bio-warfare scientist Frank Olson died in 1953 after falling from a ninth-floor window of the Hotel Pennsylvania, New York. Was it drug-induced suicide or a CIA elimination after Olson took part in MK-Ultra trials and became seriously disturbed?

Above: 1960s drug culture popularized "magic mushrooms", from which psilocybin was synthesized by Swiss scientist Albert Hoffman. He also first extracted LSD (seen here on a sugar lump) from ergot rye fungus. Both drugs are hallucinogenic.

MK-ULTRA MIND CONTROL

How better to win a war than to gain control of the minds of the enemy? That was the aim of the secret MK-Ultra human research program into behavior modification, run by the CIA's Scientific Intelligence Division in the 1950s and 60s.

The project came about partly as a response to communist claims during the Korean War that U.S. prisoners of war in North Korea had been "brainwashed" into expressing sympathy for communism. It was also born of the CIA's growing frustration at not being able to penetrate the Iron Curtain with agents and from fear of communist enemies within. The MK-Ultra project was headed by CIA chemist Sidney Gottlieb, known as the "Black Sorcerer" for his skill in preparing lethal poisons. Under Gottlieb's direction, the MK-Ultra team sought to develop mind-control drugs to counter communist brainwashing. They also wanted to be able to program individuals to carry secrets of which they were unaware—until "woken." Trial participants were unwittingly subjected to drugs such as LSD, as well as hypnosis, sensory deprivation, torture, sexual and verbal abuse and enforced isolation.

Above: Conspiracy theorists believe LSD was secretly tested on prostitutes and drug addicts, who were picked up from bars in San Francisco and taken to safe houses. This was part of the CIA plan to create a drug-culture "weapon."

Below: U.S. Senator Frank Church headed the 1975 Committee that brought the whole MK-Ultra issue to public attention.

Below: Scottish-born D. Ewen Cameron, a psychiatrist on the MK-Ultra program, is alleged to have used electric-therapy and LSD in human trials, with shocking effects.

Above: Richard M. Helms was U.S. Director of Central Intelligence from 1966 to 1973, the year he ordered MK-Ultra documents to be destroyed.

MK-Ultra's extreme methods were used on individuals to promote dependence, illogical and impulsive thinking, cause amnesia and mental confusion and to make sure a person would not "confess" under interrogation. The research was undertaken at colleges and universities, hospitals, prisons and pharmaceutical companies, sometimes knowingly, at other times through CIA "front organizations."

In 1973, with the Watergate scandal unfolding and the unpopularity of the Vietnam War to the fore, CIA director Richard Helms ordered the destruction of all MK-Ultra files in an attempt to conceal any evidence of the CIA's questionable, if not outright illegal, activities. Nevertheless, the project was brought to public attention by the Church Committee of the U.S. Congress in 1975. Then, in 1977, the Freedom of Information Act brought more information to light, and in 2001 some facts about the project were declassified.

THE TRUTH?

PRECURSORS TO MK-ULTRA WERE PROJECTS ARTICHOKE AND BLUEBIRD. THESE EVOLVED FROM OPERATION PAPERCLIP IN 1945, THE ALLIED PROGRAM TO RECRUIT NAZI SCIENTISTS AFTER GERMANY'S DEFEAT IN WORLD WAR II. AS THE COLD WAR FROZE HARDER IN THE 1950S, THE U.S. INTELLIGENCE COMMUNITY FEARED COMMUNIST USE OF MIND-CONTROL FOR SUBVERSION AND ESPIONAGE AND EMBARKED ON MK-ULTRA AS A COUNTER-MEASURE.

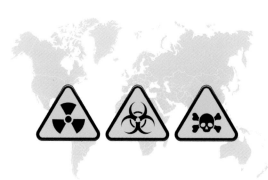

Above: Warning symbols for mass destruction, biological, chemical or nuclear, fill people with dread, but what if there are dangers high in the skies?

Above: In the 1960s, the U.S. military used aerial defoliation, spraying chemicals onto forests in Vietnam to deny the enemy cover. This was Operation Ranch Hand (1962–71).

CHEM TRAILS

Aircraft high above us leave cloud-like white trails across the sky. Could these contrails in fact be chem trails, part of a chemical conspiracy to control an unwitting population?

Airliner jet engines emit hot air into an atmosphere that, at 10,000 m (30,000 ft) or higher, is very cold. The hot gases condense to water and freeze as ice crystals, which stream out as a contrail. As well as water, contrails contain carbon dioxide and other substances, some of which, according to conspiracy theorists, are introduced for covert purposes—to control our weather, to combat global warming or even to control population growth by reducing fertility or "weeding out" the sick and aged.

Programs such as the High Frequency Active Auroral Research Program (HAARP), it's alleged, "seed" the upper atmosphere with electrically conductive materials, for weapons research or to enhance communications surveillance. Chem trails are linked back to U.S. chemical defoliation tactics in the Vietnam War in the 1960s. They are even alleged to be part of mind-control strategies, perhaps plotted by a covert new world order cabal (adding chemicals to the air to make people more docile and tractable). In addition, they are altering human evolution and are part of the worldwide cover-up of Planet X. In certain air conditions, contrails make shadows known as "black rays"—more cause for apprehension and speculation.

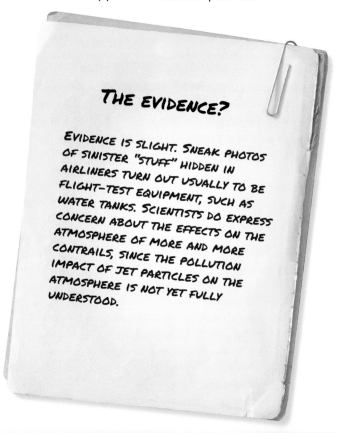

THE EVIDENCE?

EVIDENCE IS SLIGHT. SNEAK PHOTOS OF SINISTER "STUFF" HIDDEN IN AIRLINERS TURN OUT USUALLY TO BE FLIGHT-TEST EQUIPMENT, SUCH AS WATER TANKS. SCIENTISTS DO EXPRESS CONCERN ABOUT THE EFFECTS ON THE ATMOSPHERE OF MORE AND MORE CONTRAILS, SINCE THE POLLUTION IMPACT OF JET PARTICLES ON THE ATMOSPHERE IS NOT YET FULLY UNDERSTOOD.

Above: BAE's High Frequency Active Auroral Research Site (HAARP) analyses the ionosphere to investigate potential communications and surveillance enhancement. Such programs are blamed for everything from bad summers to natural disasters.

Right: Contrails in a blue sky are a familiar sight and not just around cities with busy international airports, as here in Frankfurt, Germany.

9/11

The 9/11 attacks on America in 2001 shocked the world and redirected U.S. foreign policy to a "war on terror." Controversy shrouds that fateful day. Were there other conspirators besides the al-Qaeda suicide-bombers?

Four hijacked planes crashed on 9/11. Two hit the World Trade Centre, a third hit the Pentagon. United Airlines Flight 93 crashed in Pennsylvania, after passengers fought with the hijackers. Nearly 3,000 people died. The official verdict was suicide terrorism, directed by al-Qaeda leader Osama bin Laden.

Conspiracy notions swirled among the rubble and still circulate on the web. How had skyscrapers fallen so quickly, unless blown up by demolition charges? How could hijackers fly a plane straight into the tightly-guarded Pentagon? Why were the airliners not shot down? Did President Bush know before he was told the news at a school in Sarasota, Florida? Alternative "suspects" in the web of 9/11 fantasy were: right-wing U.S. groups; Israel; China; the World Trade Center's owners; the CIA in collaboration with al-Qaeda, possibly using missiles holographically disguised as airliners; the covert New World Order; evil "Thetans" (invisible powers according to Scientologists); and gold thieves seeking bullion kept in the World Trade Centre.

Above: 50,000 people worked in the World Trade Centre, but not all were at work when, just before 8:46 am, United Airlines Flight 11 hit the North Tower. At 9:03 am, United Airlines Flight 175 struck the South Tower, shown here in flames.

Above: Rescuers help victims at the Pentagon, hit at 9:37 am by American Airlines Flight 77. Witnesses reported seeing an airliner fly into the building.

Right: This map shows the flight paths across the eastern USA of the four hijacked planes: two from Boston (11 and 175), one from New Jersey (93) and one from Washington (77).

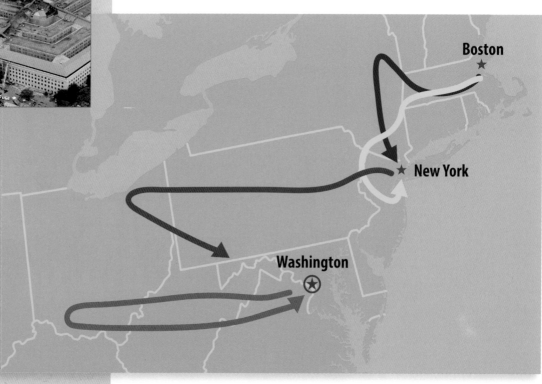

Boston

New York

Washington

Below: Firefighters and media stand at Ground Zero, in the rubble of the World Trade Centre. At 9:59 am, the South Tower collapsed, followed 29 minutes later by the North Tower. At 5:21 pm, the smaller building, known as 7 World Trade Centre, also fell.

THE TRUTH?

MANY PEOPLE SAW THE TWIN TOWERS STRUCK ON LIVE TV. FLIGHT 77'S RECORDERS AND DNA FROM VICTIMS INDICATED AIRLINER IMPACT. ON OCTOBER 7, THE U.S. AND ALLIES ATTACKED AFGHANISTAN. ALL 19 HIJACKERS WERE DEAD, BUT THEIR ACCOMPLICES WERE RIGOROUSLY PURSUED. OSAMA BIN LADEN WAS KILLED BY U.S. FORCES IN 2011.

Above: 9/11 conspiracy supporters demonstrated in Denver, Colorado, in August 2008. Conspiracy theories threw suspicion on the CIA and military. Did Wall Street have foreknowledge? Had the government staged 9/11 to justify U.S. wars in Afghanistan and Iraq?

Above: The Watergate office and apartment complex in northwest Washington DC. This insignificant building entered the lexicon of politics and cover-ups. Any "-gate" is now a scandal waiting to be disclosed.

Above: Four of the original Watergate burglars outside the U.S. District Court: Eugenio Martinez, Virgilio Gonzales (a locksmith), Bernard Baker and Frank Sturgis.

Right: On the morning of August 9, 1974, the day following President Nixon's TV resignation speech, White House Chief of Staff Alexander Haig presented this resignation letter to Nixon to sign.

WATERGATE

The biggest political scandal in modern U.S. history brought down a president. In the 1970s, "Watergate" became synonymous with "cover-up."

In 1972, U.S. election year, the Watergate building in Washington DC was the campaign HQ of the Democratic Party in its fight to deny incumbent President Richard Nixon a second term. A clumsy attempt to break in to Watergate and then cover up the burglary brought seven men, all with White House connections, to justice in January 1973. By then Nixon had been re-elected and the Watergate break-in was old news—that is, until Washington Post reporters Carl Bernstein and Bob Woodward unraveled a tale of conspiracy and cover-up.

Former White House legal aide John Dean admitted a cover-up and said Nixon knew what had gone on. The president at first refused to make public secret tapes of White House conversations and when he did, three key conversations were missing. Dogged by a Senate committee and special prosecutors, Nixon eventually released over 1,000 pages of "White House tapes," evidence of a cover-up.

Some 40 people were charged. In 1975, jail terms were handed down to senior White House insiders John Ehrlichman and H. R. Haldeman and former Attorney-General John Mitchell, for conspiracy, obstruction of justice and perjury.

Nixon faced impeachment by Congress for obstructing justice, abusing presidential powers and withholding evidence. On August 9, 1974, he resigned. He was replaced by Vice President Gerald Ford, who pardoned him for all federal crimes he might have committed.

THE WHITE HOUSE
WASHINGTON

August 9, 1974

Dear Mr. Secretary:

I hereby resign the Office of President of the United States.

Sincerely,

Richard Nixon

11.35 AM

The Honorable Henry A. Kissinger
The Secretary of State
Washington, D. C. 20520

HK

Above: Nixon's trademark grin on his presidential campaign button. His long political career ended with Watergate.

Right: Richard Nixon at a press conference as the Watergate hearings and press inquiries made him increasingly defensive.

THE TRUTH?

INFORMATION ABOUT THE COVER-UP WAS PASSED TO THE WASHINGTON POST REPORTERS BY AN ANONYMOUS WASHINGTON INSIDER, "DEEP THROAT." DEEP THROAT WAS NAMED IN 2005 AS FORMER FBI MAN MARK FELT, THOUGH OTHER CANDIDATES HAVE ALSO BEEN SUGGESTED. BOB WOODWARD SAID HE MET DEEP THROAT IN AN UNDERGROUND GARAGE, REQUESTING MEETINGS BY PUTTING FLOWER POTS WITH FLAGS ON HIS BALCONY AND RECEIVING MEETING TIMES SCRIBBLED ON HIS NEWSPAPER.

THE TRUMP FILES AND THE "BIRTHERS"

In 2011, billionaire businessman—and, since January 2017, U.S. president—Donald Trump raised concerns about America's first African-American president, Barack Obama, by questioning his place of birth. Trump's suspicions were broadcast on countless shows across the country, much to the disbelief of many.

When he appeared on NBC's *Today* show in 2011, Trump made his views known. "If he wasn't born in this country, which is a real possibility... then he's pulled one of the great cons in the history of politics," he said.

His controversial statement led to bemusement and agitation—and it gained a considerable amount of media coverage. So much so that, on April 27, 2011, President Obama released his long-form birth certificate to prove his citizenship and right to lead the country. He joked about the matter in a playful speech—with Trump in the audience—three days after its release. "No one is happier, no one is prouder, to put this birth certificate matter to rest than the Donald," he said. "And that's because he can finally get back to focusing on the issues that matter: like, did we fake the moon landing? What really happened in Roswell? And where are Biggie and Tupac?"

Following Obama's statement on the matter, Trump remained unconvinced. On August 6, 2012, he published the following tweet: "An 'extremely credible source' has called my office and told me that @Barack Obama's birth certificate is a fraud."

Following Trump's election to the presidency, CNN anchor Anderson Cooper asked Trump if he accepted that Obama's birthplace was the United States. "I really don't know. I don't know why he wouldn't release his records," he replied. "But, honestly, I don't want to get into it." In the same interview, Trump accused Hillary Clinton of being a "birther" and of initiating the controversy. However, he failed to provide any evidence of this.

Top: Many people believe the Birther conspiracy was fueled by racism and people who were unhappy to have a black man as President.

Above: Obama mocked the Birther conspiracy by claiming he had his birth video during his speech at the White House Correspondent's Dinner in 2011. He then played a clip from Disney's *The Lion King*.

TRUMPED UP: OTHER CONSPIRACY THEORIES RELATED TO TRUMP

• On November 6, 2012, Trump tweeted: "The concept of global warming was created by and for the Chinese in order to make U.S. manufacturing non-competitive."

• One rumored security claim includes lurid details from Trump's visit in 2013 to Moscow for the *Miss Universe* beauty pageant. It says Russia's FSB spy agency obtained compromising material, known as kompromat, from the hotel suite. "FSB has compromised Trump through his activities in Moscow sufficiently to be able to blackmail him," it alleged.

• Trump and his supporters accused anti-Trump rally campaigners of being professionally paid protesters.

• Trump supporters accused rival Ted Cruz of being infamous serial murderer the zodiac killer in an attempt to discredit him.

Below: Obama did release his birth certificate, however this did not stop people claiming he was not born in the USA, saying the certificate was a forgery.

Above and Left: Trump and Clinton make speeches during their electoral campaign.

ELECTION RIGGED (AGAINST TRUMP)

Above: President Vladimir Putin of Russia was often named as someone who would benefit from Trump being elected.

Although views on President Trump remain divided, it is difficult to deny that he has shaken up global politics as we know it. In October 2016, a mere three weeks before voting day, Trump tweeted the following: "The election is absolutely being rigged by the dishonest and distorted media, but also at many polling places." The claims didn't stop there. At a Wisconsin rally during his campaign trail, Trump made the following statement to his supporters: "They even want to try and rig the election at the polling booths, where so many cities are corrupt and voter fraud is all too common."

However, one of Trump's long-standing Republican rivals, Florida senator Marco Rubio, dismissed Trump's conspiracy claims. He said: "There is no evidence behind any of this, so this should not continue to be said."

On November 8, 2016, three weeks after the accusations were made, Trump won the presidential election, despite receiving almost three million fewer votes than his opponent, Hillary Clinton. However, not satisfied with the victory, he made the claim that Clinton only won the popular vote because many people residing in America illegally cast illegitimate votes.

ELECTION RIGGED (FOR TRUMP)

Since Trump became president, there have been numerous claims and rumors relating to possible Russian involvement in the 2016 U.S. presidential election. According to U.S. intelligence officials, Russian hackers made repeated attempts before and during the election campaign to get into major U.S. institutions, including the White House and the Democratic Party, to aid Trump's victory. Possible motivation, it was alleged, included Putin's disregard for Clinton and the notion that Trump was Russia's favored candidate due to his alleged "compromising" by Russian security forces.

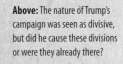

Above: The nature of Trump's campaign was seen as divisive, but did he cause these divisions or were they already there?

Left: During the 2016 campaign, Marco Rubio was a harsh critic of Trump, but by 2020 he had become a strong supporter of his former opponent.

MORGUE EMPLOYEE CREMATED BY MISTAKE WHILE TAKING A NAP!

Above and below: Other fake news headlines include a CIA Agent confessing to assassinating Marilyn Monroe on his deathbed, and an elderly woman training her cats to steal from her neighbors!

DRUNK DEMOLITION WORKER ARRESTED AFTER BLOWING UP THE WRONG BUILDING

KIM KARDASHIAN AND KANYE WEST ARE SPLITTING UP!!

WHEN ELLE MAGAZINE U.S. FALSELY REPORTED, "KIM KARDASHIAN AND KANYE WEST ARE SPLITTING UP," READERS WHO CLICKED THE LINK WERE TAKEN STRAIGHT TO A VOTER REGISTRATION SITE FOR REGISTERING TO VOTE IN THE U.S. MIDTERM ELECTIONS. THIS METHOD OF USING CELEBRITY CLICKBAIT TO MASK A POLITICAL OBJECTIVE WAS WIDELY CONDEMNED.

FAKE NEWS

Popularized by President Donald Trump, the term "fake news" has itself become news. Real news.

A phenomenon that grew in prominence in 2016, fake news stories have since flooded the internet via social media sites such as Facebook and Twitter. Sometimes shamelessly posing as real news, fake news items are often designed to provoke indignation or anger in a specific political group, sometimes targeting key demographics through data mining of social media.

So, where does fake news come from? Sometimes it can start accidentally, such as when newspaper columnist Marina Hyde sarcastically tweeted that Melania Trump had been replaced by a body double, and found it picked up by news agencies. This conspiracy gained further traction when Melania disappeared from the public eye for more than three weeks in 2018, followed by a statement later saying she had been in hospital. Not everyone was convinced, however, and the twitter hashtag #wheresmelania was still being used nearly a year later.

Other stories are started intentionally, with many sources using salacious celebrity rumor or controversial topics to drive traffic to their websites to profit from advertising revenue. These include claims that Avril Lavigne has been replaced by a look-alike, Miley Cyrus has applied for British Citizenship, or that various celebrities—including Sylvester Stallone, Morgan Freeman and Paul McCartney—have died suddenly. The last is easily solved by the celebrities in question coming forward to prove they're still alive, but it's not so easy to prove that Avril Lavigne isn't really a model called Melissa Vandella.

Above: Data taken from social media profiles allowed companies to target fake news to specific demographics, tailoring stories to the audience.

ATTACK OF THE SQUIRRELS

A well-known fake news site called the *World News Daily Report* published an article claiming that a woman had trained squirrels to attack her former lover. There was no truth to the story, but the story itself provides some insights into the murky world of fake news. *World News Daily Report* used a police photo of a real woman who was convicted of a crime, but the name the website gave for the woman had been changed, as had the details of the crime. Her real crime had been throwing bricks at a window.

The disclaimer used by the website is as follows: "WNDR assumes however all responsibility for the satirical nature of its articles and for the fictional nature of their content. All characters appearing in the articles in this website—even those based on real people—are entirely fictional and any resemblance between them and any persons, living, dead, or undead is purely a miracle." The website claims to be satirical, like comedy news sites such as *The Daily Mash* or *The Onion*—obviously the stories were clearly too bizarre to be believed, weren't they?

DAILY NEWS

WORLD · BUSINESS · SPORT · LIFESTYLE · TRAVEL · WEATHER

THE WORLD'S BEST SELLING NATIONAL NEWSPAPER

WOMAN ARRESTED FOR TRAINING SQUIRRELS TO ATTACK HER EX-BOYFRIEND

Above and below: Fake news can go from small scale to the highest offices in the world. Often stories use photographs of real people to illustrate false reports of squirrel-based assault.

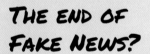

THE END OF FAKE NEWS?

IN THE LIGHT OF A PUBLIC OUTCRY AND LEGAL INQUIRIES IN THE U.S. AS TO HOW FAKE NEWS WAS AFFECTING POLITICAL OUTCOMES, FACEBOOK FOUNDER MARK ZUCKERBERG AND OTHER SOCIAL MEDIA GIANTS HAVE STARTED INVESTIGATING WAYS TO IDENTIFY AND REMOVE FAKE NEWS, OR TO STOP IT SPREADING. CYNICS SUGGEST THAT THIS IS JUST A WAY TO COMPENSATE FOR THE DATA MINING, WHICH ALLOWED FAKE NEWS TO TARGET SPECIFIC USERS BASED ON THEIR PROFILE INFORMATION, DATA WHICH HAD BEEN PROVIDED BY SOCIAL MEDIA TO THIRD PARTIES SUCH AS CAMBRIDGE ANALYTICA.

ORGANIZATIONS LIKE SNOPES.COM ARE ALSO AIMED AT IDENTIFYING AND DEBUNKING FAKE NEWS ON THE INTERNET. FOUNDED IN 1994 TO INVESTIGATE URBAN MYTHS, SNOPES IS NOW THE OLDEST AND MOST ESTABLISHED FACT-CHECKING WEBSITE ON THE INTERNET, VERIFIED BY THE INTERNATIONAL FACT CHECKING NETWORK.

WHEN FAKE NEWS IS NOT FAKE NEWS

In a complicated twist of events, however, the phrase "fake news" has also come to be used as a convenient way to deny criticisms and allegations that might be well founded. In an ongoing battle with pro-Democratic media groups in the USA, President Donald Trump famously slammed respected CNN reporter Jim Acosta with the words "You are fake news." Acosta also had his press pass revoked, barring him from White House press briefings. Freedom of the press is important for ensuring government accountability, but when the government questions the validity of the press, who can we believe?

MOON LANDING

"Houston, Tranquility Base here. The Eagle has landed." **Millions of people around the world listened and watched on TV as U.S. astronaut Neil Armstrong stepped down on to the surface of the Moon. But had the Eagle really landed on the Moon—or on a film set?**

Skeptics suggest the Moon landing never happened. They claim that after technical problems threatened the project, NASA staged an elaborate hoax in great secrecy to fulfill President Kennedy's 1961 vow to Congress. Kennedy had called for the United States to commit know-how, manpower, and limitless cash to "landing a man on the Moon and returning him safely to Earth" before the decade was over. Given the risks of a spaceflight beyond Earth orbit, skeptics argue, it was safer to win the space race by deception. It was important not to fail, to beat the Russians and to distract the U.S. public from the unpopular Vietnam War.

Conspiracy theorists point to apparent anomalies on the film footage of the Apollo astronauts, such as "camera crosshairs" on Moon rocks, the Stars and Stripes flag seemingly "ruffled" by air currents, the lack of visible stars in the lunar sky and aberrant shadows. This "proves" the astronauts were in a film studio, they argue and the Moonscape was just a painted background. It was all faked.

Above: President Kennedy gave a speech to Congress in 1961 declaring his intention to land a man on the Moon.

Above: Apollo 11 astronauts rehearsed their landing procedures at NASA's Manned Spacecraft Centre. Conspiracy theorists say similar sets were used to make the film of the Moon landing.

EVIDENCE

NO VISIBLE STARS ARE SEEN IN APOLLO PHOTOS BECAUSE THE LANDINGS TOOK PLACE DURING THE BRIGHT LUNAR DAY, AND NEIL ARMSTRONG'S FIRST STEP ON LUNAR SOIL WAS FILMED BY A CAMERA ON THE LANDER, NOT BY A HOLLYWOOD FILM CREW. EVIDENCE FROM SPACE SUGGESTS THE TRUTH.

Left: Evidence against? No stars visible in the Moon's sky. Most scientists point out that this "blackout" is quite normal.

Left: Evidence against? Too much light glare on the back pack, suggesting a studio set-up. Or is it reflected light from the Moon's surface?

Left: Evidence against? No visible blast marks or disturbance from rocket propulsion made during landing.

Below: Apollo 17 astronaut Harrison Schmitt runs across the desolate surface of the Moon. This panoramic view was compiled from lunar photographs taken in 1972.

NEW HI RES PHOTOS RELEASED BY NASA TO QUELL THEORIES

In 2017, NASA released more than 10,000 high resolution images from the Moon landings, in an attempt to put an end to rumors and conspiracy theories. Images from the organization's archives covering all 11 manned Moon missions have included spectacular shots not seen before. The images were posted to a Flickr account called Project Apollo Archive.

The photos, taken by astronauts using Hasselblad cameras, were first digitized in order to produce the clearest, sharpest resolutions. Some of the images had been seen before, but the new resolution meant they were significantly more detailed.

Left: Apollo 11's lunar laser ranging experiment package was left on the Moon. Signals reflected from it have been picked up on Earth.

Above: This photograph released by NASA clearly shows the Apollo 12 Lunar Module landing on the Moon's surface. The photograph was taken by Astronaut Richard Gordon from the orbiting Command Module.

Could such a hoax be possible, even staged by film director Stanley Kubrick (of *2001* fame)? That Apollo 11 had reached the Moon was disputed by the Flat Earth Society and by some Hindus, who said the Moon was much too far away. Propagandists in Russia and Cuba insisted that Soviet cosmonauts got to the Moon first. The "fake" claims presuppose that the astronauts lied and that 40,000 or more NASA employees were in on the deception. Third-party evidence (not from NASA, the U.S. government or conspiracy theorists) includes photos taken by spacecraft, the existence of Moon rocks (382 kg/842 pounds) from six Apollo missions and evidence that Apollo equipment is still on the Moon.

Right: A camera from Surveyor 3, a U.S. robot craft that landed on the Moon in 1967, was returned to Earth by Apollo 12. There was evidence it had been on the Moon.

THE TRUTH?

THE MOST COMPELLING EVIDENCE THAT THE APOLLO MOON LANDINGS DID TAKE PLACE COMES FROM RECENT FLY-BY OBSERVATIONS OF THE LANDING SITES BY UNMANNED PROBES. FLYING ABOVE THE SITES, THE CAMERAS REVEALED THE PRESENCE OF THE LANDERS AND OTHER EQUIPMENT LEFT BY THE APOLLO CREWS. THE APOLLO LANDERS APPEAR TO BE ON THE MOON, TO BE CHECKED OUT IF AND WHEN FUTURE ASTRONAUTS REVISIT—OR ARE THEY?

Above: The launch of Japan's lunar orbiter SELENE ("Kaguya") in 2007. Its photos of the Apollo 15 landing site showed dust-scatter from when the U.S. craft left the Moon in 1971.

ALL THINGS ALIEN

Are we alone or has the future already arrived in an alien spacecraft? Most conspiracy theories have their roots in the belief that controlling forces, usually government or quasi-government bodies, are pulling the strings.

However, a mass of speculation suggests that the conspiracy is literally out of this world—that aliens have been visiting Earth for thousands of years, are still doing so, and have secret contacts with government. It's alleged that real spacecraft, dead aliens, and even real-life ETs, are hidden away at secret locations. Crop circles appear in particular places around the world, occasionally accompanied by reports of sightings of lights in the sky. Some people claim feeling a strange energy at the site of these geometric patterns, while others claim that they're an elaborate hoax. Stranger still are the claims that the pyramids were orchestrated or even built by alien visitors. Could it really all be down to visitors from other worlds?

HAVE ALIENS WALKED ON EARTH?

Did extraterrestrials visit Earth in ancient times? Science says not. But ET theorists point to "evidence" from antiquity as well as more recent close encounters.

Supporters of the "aliens came here long ago" theory point to ancient stories of gods flying in fiery chariots and to pictures of ancient rulers in strange garb and headdress, said to be aliens in spacesuits. Extraterrestrial visitors arrived with advanced technology to observe Earth and perhaps genetically modify its life-forms. They helpfully passed on some basic technology—such as teaching the Sumerians agriculture and maths. They also helped build the Pyramids and Stonehenge.

This theory presupposes that intelligent life exists elsewhere in the universe. In the 1960s, astrophysicists I. S. Shklovski and Carl Sagan, serious scientists and essentially skeptics, judged that extraterrestrials were "possible but not proven." Erich Von Daniken on the other hand claimed much "evidence" for alien visitors in the art, religion and folklore of many cultures. Zecharia Sitchkin went further, suggesting aliens produced modern humans from a distant planet called Nibiru. They flew to Earth for minerals and genetically engineered the primitive primates they found here to make intelligent workers. When the aliens left discomfited by natural disasters and the last Ice Age, humans took over.

In 1952, George Adamski said he met a man from Venus in the Colorado Desert of California. The alien, who had long blonde hair, used telepathy to talk to Adamski and invited him on a trip to Venus in his flying saucer. Adamski was not alone; others too claim to have met aliens, who visit from planets near and far.

Above: A model of the Viking lander that visited Mars in 1976. Subsequent landings have failed to provide clear evidence of life on Mars – though some conspiracy theorists claim positive findings have been concealed.

Below: Jupiter's 4th largest moon, Europa. It is possible Europa had oceans in its past and maybe still has liquid water trapped beneath thick ice on its surface and so perhaps life-forms, too.

EVIDENCE

SCIENTISTS BELIEVE VENUS TO BE HOSTILE TO LIFE, THOUGH ADAMSKI CLAIMED HIS VENUSIANS LIVED SAFELY UNDERGROUND. ADAMSKI DID NOT BELIEVE THE FIRST-EVER PHOTOS OF THE BARREN FAR SIDE OF THE MOON, TAKEN IN 1959 BY A SOVIET SPACECRAFT, SAYING THEY'D BEEN FAKED TO HIDE THE ALIEN CITIES THAT WERE REALLY THERE. LIFE OF SOME KIND MIGHT EXIST ON MARS, BUT BACTERIA ARE UNLIKELY TO BE UP TO BUILDING SPACECRAFT TO VISIT EARTH!

Left: This is what a "scout craft" from Venus looked like, according to George Adamski, who claimed he met visitors from Venus in the 1950s.

▶ 50

Below: The Pyramids of Egypt and the ancient stones at Stonehenge in England. Are these marvels of human ingenuity in a pre-machine age or could they be evidence that aliens arrived to "engineer" human civilization?

WHO BUILT THE PYRAMIDS?

There are more than 30 pyramids in Egypt. The most famous are the three great pyramids at Ghiza, built about 4,500 years ago as royal tombs. However, conspiracy theories suggest that a veil of secrecy hides the true origin of these mighty stone marvels.

Skeptics doubt official explanations of how the pyramids were built, questioning how massive stones could have been moved and assembled with such geometric precision using manpower alone. Solar and stellar alignment of the pyramids suggests Egyptian engineers were able to calculate the year-length exactly, at 365.25 days. Was such science possible without extraterrestrial help or guidance from some other more advanced civilization—perhaps the lost world of Atlantis? Ancient Egypt's myth-laden rituals, exotic gods, complex hieroglyphics and monumental architecture fascinate historians, but are also seen by some conspiracists as evidence that our history has been shaped by alien contact. The notion that the Egyptian cosmic-view, with its sky gods and solar boats, was inspired by contact with aliens has spawned a host of theories, most alleging that the academic and political establishment covers up the evidence.

Above: In 1993, Dr. Zahi Hawass, in charge of Egypt's antiquities, closed the Great Pyramid of King Khufu for a year. Conspiracy theorists suspected the public were shut out so new, "other-worldly" finds could be examined and concealed from the media.

Above: A robot with a camera similar to this fiber-optic "snake" was sent into one of the narrow ventilation shafts deep inside the Great Pyramid. The camera recorded two mysterious doors with metal "handles". What lies behind the inner door is still a mystery.

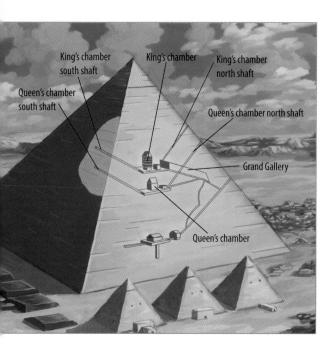

King's chamber south shaft
King's chamber
King's chamber north shaft
Queen's chamber south shaft
Queen's chamber north shaft
Grand Gallery
Queen's chamber

Above: This cutaway plan shows the interior of the Great Pyramid, with its passages, chambers and ventilation shafts. Hieroglyphs were found in a secret chamber in the Queen's chamber south shaft.

THE TRUTH?

CLOSING THE GREAT PYRAMID LED TO SPECULATION THAT EGYPTOLOGISTS WERE HIDING NEWLY FOUND EVIDENCE OF A LOST CIVILIZATION OR CONTACT. HOWEVER, VISITORS DO ERODE THE FABRIC OF ANCIENT MONUMENTS AND CAN AFFECT AIR HUMIDITY, SO ROUTINE CLOSURE FOR CLEANING AND CONSERVATION IS NOT UNUSUAL.

Below: The sun at its summer solstice sets precisely between the two biggest pyramids when seen from the Sphinx. Was this alignment achieved with alien help? Could Egyptian fascination with the sun and the cosmos be linked to contact with visitors from other worlds?

Above: The Sphinx is an enigmatic monolith, with grooves (inset) that some people argue were caused by rainwater. If that were the case, the rock could possibly date from a time long before the pyramids were built, when the climate in Egypt was less arid.

Below: The pyramids today attract visitors from all over the world. So awe-inspiring are they that some people find it hard to believe they were built by toiling desert workers alone. Were they perhaps helped by aliens using advanced technology?

CROP CIRCLES

What makes circular patterns in wheat fields? Some people like to believe that UFOs are responsible. Others suggest they are the work of followers of ancient religions, while some are simply made by artistic hoaxers.

Crop circles are geometric patterns, sometimes intricate and very large (over 200 m/650 ft) across. They are best seen from the air.

Formations that looked regular, even artistic, were first seen in fields of cereal crops in the 1970s. At first, they were associated with UFO landings or with unexplained other-worldly phenomena. Was it significant that so many crop circles were made in the ritual landscape of England, close to the ancient Bronze Age sites of Stonehenge and Avebury? However, similar phenomena have been reported in other countries. In Indonesia, crop circles were ruled to be "pseudoscience" (and so possibly alien), while the Australians blamed wallabies running in circles after grazing on opium-rich poppies!

Significantly, crop circles do not appear in medieval folklore, nor in Victorian scientists' accounts of rural beliefs and old customs. In the 1980s, meteorologists speculated that freak winds could flatten crops by "vortex-action". Ufologists claimed crop circles were made by alien spacecraft, possibly in an attempt to communicate. Another theory suggested crop circles were the Earth "talking to us"—an expression of a mysterious "Earth force," as yet unknown to science.

Human hoaxers are, however, the most obvious cause of crop circles. Two chief suspects, Doug Bower and Dave Chorley, claimed they started making circles in England in 1978 and went on to create over 200. Soon crop formations were seen in other countries. Since the 1980s there have been crop-circle competitions and even TV demonstrations of how to make one!

Above: ET just landed. This drawing of "an alien spaceship spotted making crop circles" was sent to UK government military experts to examine in the late 1990s.

Below: Best seen from the air, this crop formation was photographed in Mammendorf, Bavaria.

Left: Some crop formation designs are intricate and precise, like this one from Canton Bern, Switzerland.

EVIDENCE

The Nazca lines in Peru are best seen from the air, yet were made between 100 BCE and AD 800, long before aircraft. On the ground can be seen giant figures of spiders, fish, lizards and other animals, as well as geometric shapes. Why did the Nazca people draw them with such precision and effort? Possibly they wanted to communicate with sky-gods, or they may have been fertility symbols or calendars.

Above: Crop circle artists made this spectacular crop circle in Dorset, England.

To make a crop circle, you need a wooden board to flatten the wheat-stalks (and a farmer's permission!). The board is tied to a rope fastened to a pole, as an anchor, around which the circle-artist describes arcs to make circles and patterns. Despite demonstrations of the technique, many people prefer to believe that the patterns have some deep meaning.

THE ROSWELL INCIDENT

Probably the most-discussed "alien landing" incident was in 1947. Did aliens die in the desert of New Mexico?

In July 1947, a rancher in Roswell, New Mexico, USA, found metal debris on the ground. Was it a plane crash, or something other-worldly? America was gripped by "flying saucer fever," and the local newspaper headlined the startling news that the military had "captured a flying saucer." A press release mentioning a "flying disk" was swiftly dismissed with a counter-statement that the debris came from a weather balloon that had met with a mishap.

The balloon story, though, seemed to some to be a clumsy cover-up for a more fantastic truth. Not only had an alien spacecraft crashed, but its alien crew had been recovered and spirited away. Witnesses spoke of gouges in the desert, made by a craft crashing and UFO-converts speculated that military radar signals had messed up the alien craft's control systems. The Roswell aliens became part of UFO-mythology, with a mortician claiming to have helped with post-mortems and in 1995 a video clip on the Internet showing the actual "autopsy" of a Roswell alien—a humanoid biped of the kind known in extraterrestrial-watching circles as a "gray."

The authorities were adamant: there was no Roswell space crash and no alien corpses being preserved under guard in military freezers. The U.S. Air Force insists to this day that there is "absolutely no evidence that a spaceship crashed near Roswell" or that any dead aliens were recovered.

Above: Khrushchev and Kennedy meet in the 1960s. Both sides claimed the other was testing secret weapons.

EVIDENCE?

CONSPIRACY THEORISTS WERE EXCITED BY A MEMO RELEASED IN 2011 UNDER U.S. FREEDOM OF INFORMATION LAW. SENT IN MARCH 1950 BY AN FBI AGENT, IT CLAIMED "THREE SO-CALLED FLYING SAUCERS HAD BEEN RECOVERED," EACH WITH THREE BODIES "OF HUMAN SHAPE BUT ONLY [0.9 M] 3 FEET TALL" AND WEARING PRESSURE SUITS. THIS MEMO MIGHT SEEM TO SHORTEN THE ODDS ON THE ROSWELL ALIENS BEING REAL, BUT IT'S ALMOST CERTAINLY A HOAX.

Right: Newspapers reported investigations into the strange crash, but the U.S. Military released a statement saying that the craft was a weather balloon.

Disk Craze Continues

Army Disk-ounts New Mexico Find As Weather Gear

FORT WORTH, July 9.—(AP)—An examination by the Army revealed last night that a mysterious object found on a lonely New Mexico ranch was a harmless high-altitude weather balloon—not a grounded flying disk.

Excitement was high in disk-conscious Texas until Brig Gen. Roger M. Ramey, commander of the Eight Air Forces with headquarters here cleared up the mystery.

The bundle of tinfoil, broken wood beams and rubber remnants of a ballon was sent here yesterday by army air transport in the wake of reports that it was a flying disk.

But the general said the objects were the crushed remains of a Ray wind target used to determine the direction and velocity of winds at high altitudes.

Warrant Officer Irving Newton, forecaster at the Army Air Forces weather station here, said "we use them because they go much higher than the eye can see."

NOT A FLYING DISC—Major Jesse A. Marcel of Houma, La., intelligence officer of the 509th Bomb Group at Roswell, New Mexico, inspects what was identified by a Fort Worth, Texas, Army Air Base weather forecaster as a ray wind target used to determine the direction and velocity of winds at high altitudes. Initial stories originating from Roswell, where the object was found, had labelled it a "flying disc" but inspection at Fort Worth revealed its true nature.

LOST PURSE HOLDING DIAMONDS IS FOUND, BUT MONEY MISSING

Below: This 1956 UFO book advertisement suggests that UFO witnesses had been gagged by the authorities.

Why were these men SILENCED?

They Knew Too Much About Flying Saucers

One by one, the leading figures among flying saucer researchers, who have challenged the government denial that saucers come from outer space, have been silenced. They are still alive, still living where they used to. But they will no longer talk about flying saucers or reveal why they refuse to do so.

Who were the three men in dark suits that visited them? Were they government agents, or agents of other planets? Whoever they were, they have silenced the researchers.

Now . . . in THEY KNEW TOO MUCH ABOUT FLYING SAUCERS, you may read the facts behind this frightening story — facts never before published!

Gray Barker, the author, was Chief Investigator for the International Flying Saucer Bureau—an organization which had its principal leader silenced by three men in black before he could reveal to the world his solution of the flying saucer mystery. Other leading investigators have also been intimidated. All their stories are here.

Grey Barker remains one of the unsilenced few. His true, amazing report includes eye-witness accounts of the famed Flatwoods "monster" which landed on a dark West Virginia hillside.

READ

WHAT HAPPENED TO CERTAIN RESEARCHERS WHO FOUND OUT WHERE THE SAUCERS COME FROM!

UNIVERSITY BOOKS, INC. Dept. F
404 Fourth Avenue, New York 16, New York

Please send me ...... copies of THEY KNEW TOO MUCH ABOUT FLYING SAUCERS by Gray Barker.
☐ I enclose $3.50 for each, you pay postage.
☐ Please send C.O.D. I'll pay postman $3.50 for each plus C.O.D. postage.

Name..

Address..

City...

Zone.........State................................

7

Right: A sign likely to invite the curious rather than send them off in the opposite direction. Despite efforts from governments to suggest otherwise, many people still believe aliens have landed on Earth.

Below: Irving Newton, a weatherman at Roswell Army Air Field, New Mexico, holds up debris from the supposed flying saucer found at the Roswell crash site.

Over the years more ufologists have come, albeit reluctantly, to share this view. The available evidence, much of it based on hearsay and fading memories, points to a negative: no close encounter, this time. This has not, however, stopped the Roswell Incident from entering UFO folklore and from being an ongoing inspiration for creative writers and film-makers. Nothing beats a dead alien, except, of course, a live one. . .

AREA 51

A few outbuildings in the dusty Nevada desert may conceal an amazing truth—that alien visitors not only came to Earth, but are still here. Or maybe they were not aliens at all, but creatures from the future!

Area 51 has been a magnet for conspiracy theories ever since the "flying saucer" sensations of the 1940s and 50s. Even today, visiting TV crews driving along the dirt road from nearby Rachel can find themselves suddenly confronted by armed guards, who make it clear that no visitors are allowed—no trespassing, no photos permitted. In 1947, the "Roswell incident" started a long-running conspiracy theory. Lieutenant Walter Haut, base PR man at the time, put out a release explaining that the "crashed spacecraft" was just a weather balloon. But when Haut died in 2006, he left an affidavit confirming what ufologists had long claimed, that the "balloon" was a cover-story and that aliens had landed, been studied at Area 51 and were even still at Area 51. In 1987, Robert Lazar claimed that alien spacecraft were being studied and copied by reverse engineering, at an Area 51 facility known as S-4; his claims were ridiculed, along with his credibility—but that simply added more fuel to the conspiracy fire.

Above: According to microbiologist Dan Burisch, an alien creature similar to these is housed in an underground laboratory at S-4/Area 51. It is called "J-Rod" and it came from a distant star-system.

Below: This map shows the site of Area 51 and the Nellis Air Force Range. The location in the Nevada desert is about as discouraging to visitors as any secret operation could wish for.

THE TRUTH?

Is Area 51 just a collection of huts, or a time-portal? Area 51 scientist Dan Burisch claimed to have seen an alien called "J-Rod", who is telepathic, comes from 50,000 years in the future, needs medical attention and is here to recover genetic material to repair biological damage to our descendants. A mind-blowing idea. . .

Above: Area 51, close to Groom Lake and Papoose Lake, looks deserted, but any visitors are confronted by signs that warn them to keep out.

Above: Aliens continue to bring tourists to New Mexico, and local businesses play this up with kitschy themed restaurants and motels.

ALIENS IN OUR SPACE

For decades people have claimed to have seen alien spacecraft in our skies. In 2014, one was apparently identified as being based permanently right here in our solar system.

In 1947, pilot Kenneth Arnold helped ignite the modern UFO (Unidentified Flying Object) controversy. While flying near Mt Rainier in Washington state, U.S., he saw nine flying discs, each "like a saucer skipping across a lake." The name stuck and became widely used. Arnold wondered if he'd seen alien spacecraft, but skeptics argue it was a meteoroid breaking up, making fireballs in the atmosphere.

In 1948, Captain Thomas Mantell crashed in his P-51 Mustang while pursuing a mysterious object. The U.S. Air Force said he had chased after Venus and met with a tragic accident, but ufologists argued that the unlucky pilot had tangled with an alien. In 1950, in his book Flying Saucers are Real, Donald Keyhoe speculated that UFOs were probably extraterrestrial, had been visiting Earth for centuries and seemed peaceful. A typical "sighting" was in 1964, when Lonnie Zamora, a policeman in Socorro, New Mexico, saw two small "aliens" who then took off in their oval spacecraft. Witnesses said their "aliens" were like small people, with long arms and large heads.

The U.S. Air Force and other forces around the world investigated; in the United States after Project Sign and Project Grunge came Project Blue Book, with hundreds of sightings analyzed. Most were dismissed as fantasy, fraud or mistake. UFO-fans concluded the military was hiding the truth.

EVIDENCE?

PILOTS HAVE CONTINUED REPORTING UNEXPLAINED "SIGHTINGS." IN 2008, A POLICE HELICOPTER NEAR CARDIFF ALMOST COLLIDED WITH A MYSTERY CRAFT, WHICH IT CHASED AS FAR AS NORTH DEVON. THE OFFICIAL LINE REMAINS THE SAME: NO EVIDENCE THAT UFOS ARE EXTRATERRESTRIAL IN ORIGIN. IN 2009, IT WAS SUGGESTED A SECRET U.S. SPY PLANE NAMED AURORA, WHICH OFFICIALLY DOES NOT EXIST, MIGHT BE THE ORIGIN OF AT LEAST SOME UFO SIGHTINGS.

Above: Rosetta probe and comet 67P Churyumov-Gerasimenko with Philae lander on surface.

Right: The mystery plane that officially does not exist: the U.S. SR-91 Aurora.

In November 2014, the European Space Agency's Rosetta Mission successfully landed its Philae probe on a speeding comet, known as 67P. It was the first time such an amazing feat had been achieved. Immediately it was alleged that this was an ESA and NASA cover-up to disguise the comet's true nature—as an alien spaceship. Why otherwise would they spend billions of dollars on a ten-year journey to simply take photos of a random comet in space?

The civilization responsible for the spaceship had apparently been sending radio wave "messages" to NASA for 20 years, and hi-res images of the comet show a transmission tower-like structure on its surface. Ufologist Scott Waring said, "Is it a message of greeting. . . or a warning of what's to come? We need to find out." ESA's confirmation that the comet had been emitting a "mystery song" has only fueled these theories. Sadly the probe landed in the shade, so its solar panels could not recharge its batteries and it ceased transmitting data.

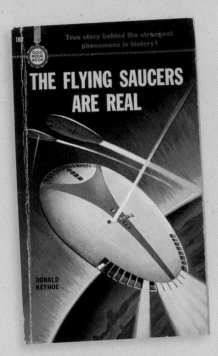

Above: This book by Donald Keyhoe was one of the earliest about UFOs, claiming that they were extraterrestrial and not from Earth.

Below: This photo, provided by the European Space Agency, shows comet 67P/CG acquired by the ROLIS instrument on the Philae lander during descent, on November 12, 2014.

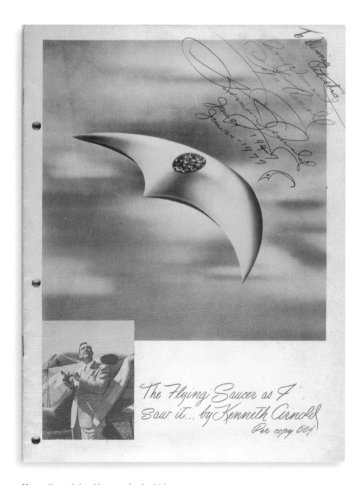

Above: Kenneth Arnold wrote a book which described his sighting of "flying saucers."

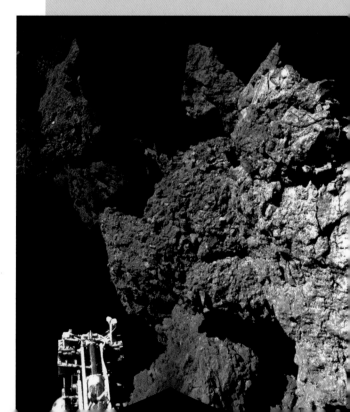

BEYOND BELIEF?

Stranger than fiction are some of the weird and wonderful "facts" that the wilder and more complex conspiracy theories promote. Some are quite harmless, but others at times threaten to spill over into religious, racial, or other forms of persecution and discrimination.

Among the more extreme ideas is the belief that secret societies (or specific groups, such as the Knights Templar) have long been dedicated to covert and subversive operations aimed at world control. Conspiracists maintain that throughout history, secret "string-pullers" have been behind all major events, including wars and revolutions. It follows that world leaders and governments are puppets manipulated by gangsters or religious fanatics. Other ideas include secrets surrounding the life of Jesus Christ or even the world being flat after all. But are they really beyond belief, or could the truth just be more than we could possibly imagine?

THE MILLENNIUM BUG

The Y2K or Year 2000 problem caused worldwide mini-hysteria. Would computers crash? If so, would the world as we know it end or at least slow down?

Computers mark time on internal clocks and calendars. Customarily, 20th-century computers abbreviated a year date to 2 digits (so 1998 = 98). As the end of the 20th century approached, what would happen to computers as the year 99 rolled over to 00? As the millennium bug popped its head above the cyber-wall, there was talk of "nasty shocks" and the "Y2K" problem. Fears were raised of "holes" in military networks, breakdowns in banking and retail, even fuel and food shortages.

As the "main event horizon," January 1, 2000, approached, the global e-community seemed split between those scared that the end of the e-world was nigh and those who dismissed the millennium bug as scaremongering, hoax or a criminal conspiracy opening the way for cyber-attacks on bank accounts. When the New Year dawned, the Y2K effect was minimal, with only minor problems, such as alarms going off, mobile phones deleting new messages instead of old ones and master clocks going wrong. The U.S. Naval Observatory clock, for instance, gave the date on its website as January 1, 19100. In the event, most computers were already Y2K-compliant and carried on. The Internet did not collapse.

The Y2K panic again showed the power of the Internet to disseminate hoax and conspiracy stories. For instance, in 1994 Internet "reports" claimed Microsoft boss Bill Gates had acquired exclusive e-rights to the Bible! In the event, the bug was no threat. Most systems were fine simply by being restarted, and by January 1, 2000, the snowball story had melted away and the e-world was still in place.

Above: In the days before January 1, 2000, the U.S. Federal Reserve was seriously worried about a flood of withdrawals by people fearful that ATMs would be hit by the Millennium Bug.

Left: In an increasingly digitized society, governments and large institutions such as hospitals were running on computers. The risks of Y2K on society were a major issue.

EVIDENCE

THE UNITED STATES PASSED AN ACT OF CONGRESS TO "BE READY" FOR Y2K PROBLEMS AND FEDERAL AGENCIES SET UP Y2K TASK FORCES. INSURANCE COMPANIES CASHED IN BY SELLING POLICIES COVERING FAILURES CAUSED BY THE BUG. GROUPS ANTICIPATING THE END OF THE WORLD STOCKED UP ON CANNED AND DRIED FOOD—JUST IN CASE THE LIGHTS WENT OUT.

Below right: Computers hold so much of our personal information. People were worried that all that data might suddenly become inaccessible or simply vanish.

FLAT EARTH THEORY REVIVED

On January 25, 2016, hip-hop artist B.o.B (Bobby Ray Simmons, Jr.) made a bold claim to his millions of followers on Twitter: that, despite what scientists have led us to believe, the earth is in fact flat.

Science's assertion of the earth's spherical nature dates back to Aristotle, around 350 BCE. However, there are a growing number of people who not only support the flat earth theory, they swear by it.

The Flat Earth Society, founded by the late Samuel Shenton in 1956, has grown in popularity since the U.S. rapper released his statement, reviving an argument that had been firmly put to bed. B.o.B's tweet was published alongside a picture of a horizon that appears completely straight. He tweeted: "The cities in the background are approx. 16 miles apart. . . where is the curve? Please explain this?" The tweet received over 3,000 likes and retweets, including a number of counterarguments as fans and followers challenged his view.

So what is the flat earth theory, and why are people making such claims about the structure of our planet? The current president of the Flat Earth Society, Daniel Shenton, explained the structure of earth as he sees it: "I see the world as being flat. It's a disc. . . there are changes in the surface, but generally it's a flat disc."

Right: The Flat Earth theory states that the world is a flat disk rather than a sphere.

Other believers have described the earth as a flat disc protected by an invisible barrier called "the firmament." When asked how gravity fits into this unscientific claim, Shenton said: "The effects of gravity, I feel, could be simulated over what people think of as a mainstream idea of gravity. [It] would be simulated by simply the disc of the earth accelerating upward at 9.8 meters per second. It would have the same effects of what people traditionally think of as gravity."

So where does that leave us today? Many esteemed scientists have spoken out about the flat earth theory and explained why the belief is implausible. American astrophysicist Neil deGrasse Tyson has highlighted numerous flaws in the theory, and in particular B.o.B's thoughts on the matter.

Tyson critiqued the rapper's statement on the inconceivable visibility of the New York City skyline. B.o.B said that if the earth were curved, then the skyline wouldn't be visible from a distance, but hidden behind 170 feet of earth. However, Tyson corrected the rapper whose miscalculations seemed to further discredit the theory. He explained that, in reality, the earth's curve blocks 150 feet of Manhattan at that distance, not 170.

Above: Depiction of a flat planet earth, with curious little wheels for the ships to go round without (hopefully) falling off into space. The UK and Europe are clearly visible, as are the African continent, India and Australia. Date: 1922.

Below: Aristotle provided evidence for the spherical shape of the Earth on empirical grounds around 330 BCE.

Above: Mary Magdalene was a follower of Christ, but it is suggested that after a feud between her and Peter, he downplayed Mary's role in the early Church, telling everyone she was a prostitute.

THE JESUS CONSPIRACY

The life of Jesus Christ is described in the Bible, but in the absence of much other historical evidence, conspiracy theorists have invented alternative biographies rather different from that taught by Christian churches.

The "Jesus Conspiracy" hypothesis suggests that Jesus had an alternative life-story, a family and a "blood-line," which led to the Merovingian royal dynasty—and beyond. The most way-out theories suggest Jesus was a descendant of Adam and Eve hybrids, created by aliens from Nibiru (aka Planet X). The Turin Shroud is said by some to be proof that Jesus was taken down from the cross alive and survived. His marriage to Mary Magdalene was covered up, some say, as the role of women in the early church was erased by later Christian writers. The Holy Grail cup, at the heart of many Jesus conspiracies, became an icon for historical crusaders—and the fictional Indiana Jones. It was said to have the power to save life, which led to a spate of quests to find the cup.

Below: The blood of Christ is central to the Christian mass or communion. Some say the Holy Grail caught the blood of Jesus as he died. Others suggest the Grail doesn't refer to a cup, but rather to the "sangreal" or "royal blood" of Jesus. It was a coded symbol to protect his bloodline.

Left: Dan Brown based his thriller, The Da Vinci Code, on the premise that Jesus left a bloodline from his relationship with Mary Magdalene. This inspired deception, feuding and murder over many centuries.

Right: Jesus Christ's influence was profound, whether or not you believe he was the son of God. Speculation about Jesus enthralls believers and non-believers alike.

Below: The New Testament of the Bible is the account of Jesus's life. The four Gospels were written many years after the crucifixion, but scholars believe other accounts were suppressed by the Church.

Right: Christians drink wine in remembrance of the Last Supper from a chalice such as this. In the quest for the Holy Grail, seekers sought a chalice (either made of gold or something more humble).

Below: A painting of the Last Supper, from a church in Brussels, Belgium. Some say the Holy Grail was the cup used at this meal.

THE TRUTH?

MOST SCHOLARS FIND NO EVIDENCE TO SUPPORT THE WILDER SPECULATIONS ABOUT JESUS, BUT CONSPIRACIES FEED THE PUBLIC APPETITE FOR SENSATIONAL "RELIGION." THAT JESUS MAY HAVE LOVED MARY MAGDALENE WAS SUGGESTED IN THE 1200s BY A MONK, PETER OF VAUX DE CERNAY. THE FINDING IN 1945 OF A 4TH-CENTURY EGYPTIAN COPTIC TEXT OF THE "GOSPEL OF PHILIP," WHICH MENTIONS A "WIFE," AROUSED FRESH INTEREST.

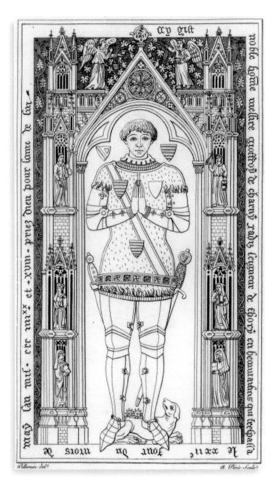

Above: The memorial brass on the tomb of Geoffroi de Charny (1300–1356), a French knight and the first authenticated owner of the Turin Shroud.

Above: This reconstruction of the tomb of Jesus includes a burial cloth. The Turin Shroud is held by some to be evidence of Christ's death and resurrection and by others to be quite the contrary.

THE TURIN SHROUD

A holy relic from the tomb of Jesus Christ or a skillful medieval fake? The Turin Shroud has kept its secret for centuries.

The Shroud is a long strip of linen cloth measuring 4.4 m (14 ft 3 in.) by 1.1 m (3 ft 7 in.). Preserved in Turin Cathedral in Italy, it is believed by some Christians to be the burial cloth in which the body of Christ was wrapped in the tomb. Its early history is itself shrouded in mystery. We know that there were reports of a sacred burial cloth in Constantinople until 1204. According to legend, the Crusaders took this shroud to France, where the first-known owner was Geoffroi de Charny, in the mid-1300s. In 1432, it was presented by his granddaughter to the Duke of Savoy. In 1532, the Shroud was damaged by fire and repaired by some nuns, and since 1578 it has been in Turin Cathedral. Interest in the Shroud's mysterious image increased after 1898, when it was first photographed. It was noticed that the negative showed a clear image of the back and front of a man, seemingly imprinted on the cloth. On examination, the body appeared to show signs of a violent death—blows to the face, bloodstains and puncture marks on the head, lash wheals on chest and abdomen, bruising and cuts on shoulders and knees and evidence of wounds in the wrists, feet and side. In 1902, it was suggested that the image was the imprint of a human body.

Many people became convinced that the Turin Shroud was a unique relic. German writer Karl Bernan suggested that the cloth marks might mean that Christ had been taken down from the cross alive and revived in the tomb—counter to Christian belief that Christ rose from the dead. Skeptics declared that the Shroud must be a forgery, but how it could have been made was a puzzle. The Catholic Church opposed scientific tests, for fear of damaging the fabric, but in the 1980s radiocarbon dating of the cloth was finally sanctioned.

Above: In 1578, a fresco of the Shroud was made by Giovanni Testa showing the Shroud on display to the Church in Turin.

Above: A replica of the kind of tomb in which Jesus was buried, as described by his followers, with the entrance stone rolled away.

Right: Detail of the head of the man whose body-image appears on the Shroud.

EVIDENCE

IN 1987, LABORATORIES IN ARIZONA, OXFORD AND ZURICH EACH TESTED SAMPLES OF CLOTH FROM THE TURIN SHROUD TO ESTABLISH ITS AGE. THEIR FINDINGS INDICATED A LIKELY DATE FOR THE LINEN OF BETWEEN 1260 AND 1390. THIS EVIDENCE SUGGESTS THE SHROUD IS MEDIEVAL AND NOT FROM THE TIME OF CHRIST 2,000 YEARS AGO.

Above: Evidence suggests that the Turin Shroud could have been woven on a Roman loom similar to this. On the other hand, an attested burial cloth from a 1st-century tomb found near Jerusalem in 2000 had a simpler weave.

Below: Pilgrims from all over the world—both clerical, like these friars, and laypeople—come to see the Turin Shroud.

Originally, it was decided that seven laboratories would test the fabric. Then the Catholic Church changed its mind and only three were permitted to: at Oxford, Zurich and Tucson. They used fragments from a single portion of the cloth. Also contrary to the agreed protocols, the labs did not test simultaneously. Critics of the date-findings suggested that the sample was a medieval repair or that the cloth samples had been contaminated (perhaps by smoke), distorting the carbon-date. Giulio Fanti, of the University of Padua, claims his thread-tests show a date from 300 BCE to AD 400, placing the Shroud from the time of Christ. Plant pollen traces in the Shroud show links to the Jerusalem area, and while science has cast doubt on the age of the cloth, if it was made in the Middle Ages, it is an amazingly clever and mystifying fake.

Above: The Vatican in Rome, the headquarters of the Catholic Church, which has protected the Turin Shroud for centuries.

Left: The image on the Shroud shows the full length of a person, not just a face. Photographs have revealed what appears to be both the back and front of a man.

THE TRUTH?

THE FINAL SAMPLE THAT WAS TAKEN MEASURED 81 x 16 MM (3.2 x 0.7 IN.). IT WAS CUT IN TWO. ONE HALF WAS STORED AND THE OTHER HALF WAS CUT INTO THREE FOR CARBON-DATING AT THE THREE LABORATORIES. THREE CONTROL SAMPLES OF TEXTILES WERE USED, WITH KNOWN DATES OF AD 200, 1100 AND 1240-1270. THE RESULTS, SUGGESTING THE SHROUD-SAMPLE HAD A MEDIEVAL ORIGIN, WERE LEAKED IN AUGUST 1988.

Above: Voltaire, the 18th-century French radical philosopher, was a Freemason. It was the secret society of choice for several notables in Europe and America in the Age of Reason.

Right: An anti-Semitic cartoon from the French La Libre Parole (1933). This journal serialized the wildly anti-Jewish libels of the "Protocols of the Elders of Zion," claiming Zionists were plotting world domination.

SECRET SOCIETIES

Secret societies are claimed to control the world. Most such beliefs are harmless, but myths and lies have on occasions led to persecution and genocide.

The Protocols of the Elders of Zion was a faked document outlining a Jewish plan for global domination. First published in Russia in 1903, it was widely translated, with Henry Ford funding 500,000 copies in the United States in the 1920s. The Protocols fueled Antisemitism at a time when Nazi leader Adolf Hitler was brooding his "final solution"—the Holocaust. The Protocols were revealed as fake in the 1920s, but are still peddled as authentic.

Freemasons, with their secret rituals and symbols, were suspected of conspiracy from the 1700s. Prominent 18th-century Masons included Benjamin Franklin, Mozart, Voltaire and George Washington. Despite their fraternal and charitable ideals, Masons were accused of plotting the American and French Revolutions, the Jack the Ripper killings and the downfall of conventional religion. Fears of a "Masonic conspiracy" in the United States gave rise in the 1820s to a political party, the Anti-Masonic Party.

Wacky and best-selling writers connected both Freemasons and the Knights Templar (also medieval) with secret world government and devil-worship. Charges of Satanism and homosexuality brought down the Templars in the early 1300s. A Christian order of knights to protect pilgrims to Jerusalem, the Templars seemed untouchable, yet their fall was dramatic. Templars were burned at the stake by the French king, but their legacy inspired a host of fantasy-writers.

U.S. conspiracy theorist and academic Carroll Quigley (1910–77) suggested that throughout history "secret societies rule," and that a British imperial secret society founded in 1891 by Cecil Rhodes and Alfred Lord Milner has continued ever since under various names, including the Royal Institute of International Affairs.

The Gemstone File hypothesis suggests Greek billionaire Aristotle Onassis was behind a worldwide conspiracy involving Joseph Kennedy (father of the president) and the Mafia. The Mafia and other groups, such as the Japanese Yakuza, have long been rumored to control governments and corporations, having moved from street crime to the bigger profits of the boardroom.

Above: Jackie Kennedy-Onassis with husband Aristotle Onassis in 1974. Greek shipping magnate Onassis was suspected by some conspiracy theorists to be a "Mr Big" in a covert clique of global power-brokers.

Below: The symbol of the eye within a triangle is known as the Eye of Providence, and has ties to Christian iconography. It is also associated with the Illuminati.

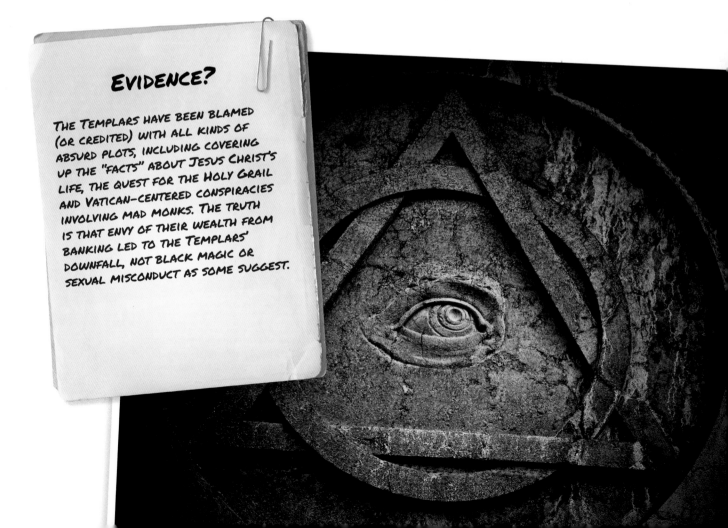

EVIDENCE?

THE TEMPLARS HAVE BEEN BLAMED (OR CREDITED) WITH ALL KINDS OF ABSURD PLOTS, INCLUDING COVERING UP THE "FACTS" ABOUT JESUS CHRIST'S LIFE, THE QUEST FOR THE HOLY GRAIL AND VATICAN-CENTERED CONSPIRACIES INVOLVING MAD MONKS. THE TRUTH IS THAT ENVY OF THEIR WEALTH FROM BANKING LED TO THE TEMPLARS' DOWNFALL, NOT BLACK MAGIC OR SEXUAL MISCONDUCT AS SOME SUGGEST.

THE ILLUMINATI

The Illuminati ("the enlightened") were a group of 18th-century intellectuals, but if conspiracy theorists are correct, they became a secret worldwide organization.

Popularized in books such as Dan Brown's Angels and Demons, the Illuminati are said to have been behind the French Revolution, Wellington's victory at Waterloo in 1815, and John Kennedy's assassination in 1963. Organized tightly like the Jesuits, it's claimed they even replaced George Washington. Their plan is to institute the new world order—a "world government"—and they adopted the Egyptian pyramid and the "all-seeing eye" as symbols. Revolutions and politics were masterminded by the Illuminati, whose members included the composer Mozart, Jewish financiers and a string of world leaders, from Garibaldi and Lenin to modern heads of state. The Illuminati are said to control the economy and media, including the movie industry. Killing anyone who opposes them, be they popes or presidents, is all part of their long-term business plan.

Above: Adam Weishaupt (1748–1830), German rationalist and freemason, founded the Illuminati in 1776 and allegedly took the murdered Washington's place as U.S. President. He told his fellow-Illuminati, "Devote yourselves to the art of deception".

Above: The Eye of Providence symbol appears on the logo of the U.S. Information Awareness Office and on the reverse of the U.S. Great Seal and dollar bill.

Above: In this re-enactment, French cavalry ride to battle at Waterloo in 1815—one of numerous key events in history supposedly "fixed" by the Illuminati.

THE TRUTH?

THE ILLUMINATI BEGAN IN GERMANY IN 1776. ITS MEMBERS WERE INFLUENCED BY A MIX OF RATIONALISM, THE OCCULT, ANTI-CATHOLICISM, SECRECY AND FREEMASONRY. BY 1784, THE ORDER HAD 3,000 MEMBERS ACROSS EUROPE.

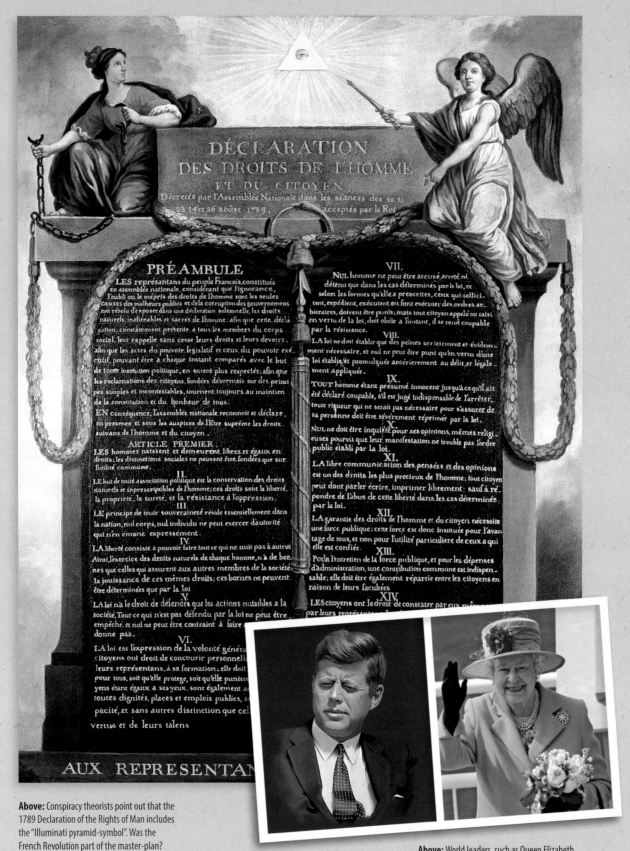

Above: Conspiracy theorists point out that the 1789 Declaration of the Rights of Man includes the "Illuminati pyramid-symbol". Was the French Revolution part of the master-plan?

Above: World leaders, such as Queen Elizabeth II, allegedly owe their position to the Illuminati, who eliminate opposition, like assassinated U.S. President Kennedy.

NEW WORLD ORDER

Some people believe that secretive New World Order leaders are plotting global control. Through wars, our nation states will be abolished and people will be ruled by propaganda and mind-control. The New World Order would slash the world's population and bring back a feudal system (lords on top, peasants at the bottom).

In 2014–15, a major outbreak of the deadly ebola virus occurred in west Africa. New World Order theorists say this terrible event was organized deliberately, as a means of global population control. As well as killing thousands, as the outbreak spread it would necessitate the implementation of travel bans, martial law and strict quarantines, all useful methods of population control. Some even claimed that when a new vaccine was introduced, people would at the same time secretly have a microchip implanted under their skin that would give the authorities control over their whereabouts and personal information.

The New World Order conspiracy is also linked to extremist groups attacking democratic institutions and to religious ideas about the second coming, Antichrist and Armageddon. The end of the world is predicted in various ways (number of popes, days in the Mayan calendar, prophesies like those of Nostradamus...). The politically-oriented New World Order is said to have evolved from the United Nations, the World Health Organization, the G8 rich nations, and the Bilderberg Group (started 1954)—an annual gathering of 100 to 150 influential persons.

Above: A truck-bomb attack on a federal government building in Oklahoma City in 1995 killed 168 and left many injured. It's alleged it was part of a far-right conspiracy to destabilize democratic government. One bomber was executed in 2001, the other given life in jail.

AT A GLANCE

THE TERM NEW WORLD ORDER DESCRIBED RECONSTRUCTION AFTER THE TWO WORLD WARS AND WAS USED IN HITLER'S THIRD REICH. IN 1940, H. G. WELLS WROTE "THE NEW WORLD ORDER", EXTOLLING A COLLECTIVIST WORLD-STATE. POST-1945, COMMUNISTS WERE NEW WORLD ORDER ARCHITECTS; TODAY'S VILLAINS ARE GLOBAL CAPITALISTS AND THE STATE MACHINE.

Right: The Great Seal of the United States carries the Latin tag "Novus Ordo Seclorum" (New Order of the Ages).

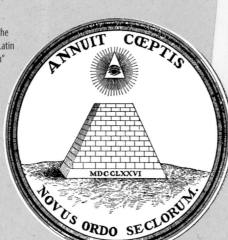

Below: Both pandemics and vaccinations are subject to conspiracy theories about population control and secret governments wanting to poison citizens.

Above: The UN flag is a symbol of hope that nations can settle disputes and live in harmony. However, the UN has not proved the world government some hoped it would be after its foundation in the 1940s.

Above: Some religious groups believe that the current world system is doomed in any case and demonstrate to urge us to prepare for the new order.

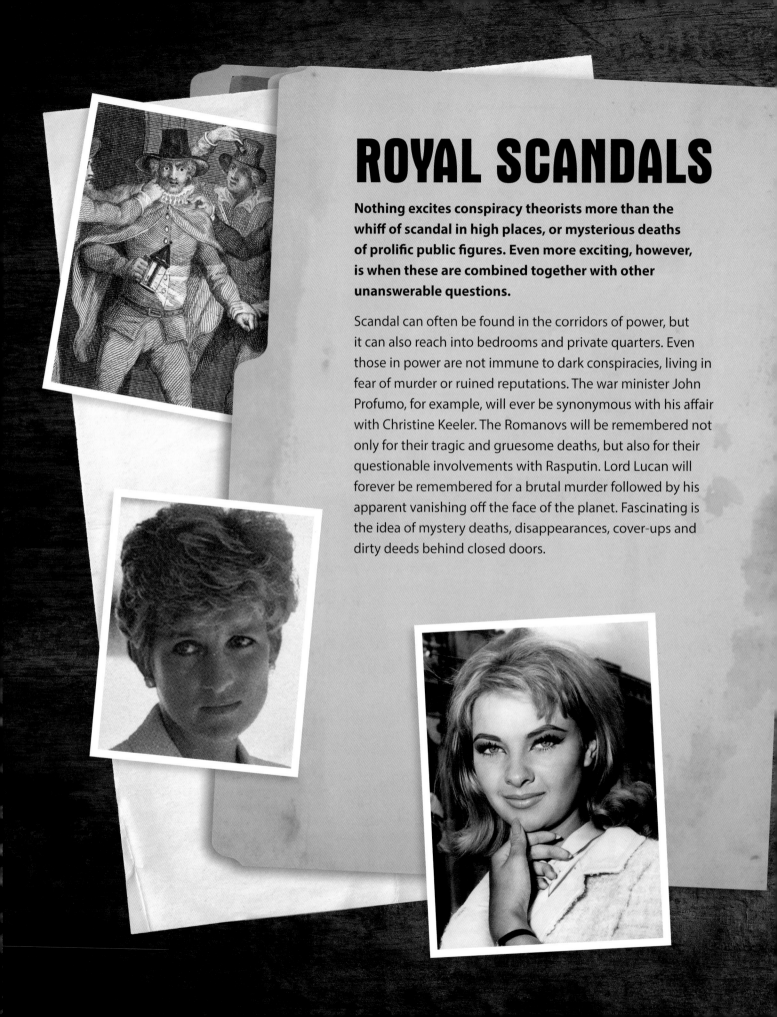

ROYAL SCANDALS

Nothing excites conspiracy theorists more than the whiff of scandal in high places, or mysterious deaths of prolific public figures. Even more exciting, however, is when these are combined together with other unanswerable questions.

Scandal can often be found in the corridors of power, but it can also reach into bedrooms and private quarters. Even those in power are not immune to dark conspiracies, living in fear of murder or ruined reputations. The war minister John Profumo, for example, will ever be synonymous with his affair with Christine Keeler. The Romanovs will be remembered not only for their tragic and gruesome deaths, but also for their questionable involvements with Rasputin. Lord Lucan will forever be remembered for a brutal murder followed by his apparent vanishing off the face of the planet. Fascinating is the idea of mystery deaths, disappearances, cover-ups and dirty deeds behind closed doors.

MURDERED MONARCHS

"Uneasy lies the head that wears a crown. . ." wrote Shakespeare. The chronicle of murdered monarchs makes grisly reading.

Above: The Tower of London, where, in 1583, the two Yorkist princes were probably murdered. What is now known as the Bloody Tower was at the time called the Garden Tower.

Kings make enemies and many kings have met violent deaths, either in battle or by an assassin's hand. Mystery surrounds the death in 1100 of William Rufus, son of the Norman William the Conqueror. He was shot while out hunting. But was it an accident or did the bowman have the king in full view? Walter Tirel was named as the culprit, but only much later.

When England's King Edward IV died, naturally, in April 1483, his son should have been crowned Edward V. However, an uncle stood in his path—and so arose the story of the Princes in the Tower. Edward V, who was only 12 years old, was taken in charge by his mother and her unpopular Woodville relatives, but decoyed away by their uncle Richard of Gloucester. He persuaded the queen to hand over both Edward and his younger brother Richard. Both boys were shut up in the Tower of London and declared illegitimate and Richard became King Richard III in July 1483.

The two princes were never seen again. Richard ruled until 1485, when he lost the Battle of Bosworth to Henry Tudor, who became Henry VII. The discovery in 2012 of Richard III's remains under a car park in Leicester, kindled renewed speculation, but there is no further evidence. Richard was reburied in Leicester Cathedral in March 2015.

Oddly, one name recurs in the stories of these deaths 400 years apart: Tirel/Tyrrell. Tudor historians blamed Sir James Tyrrell as the Princes' chief assassin. Bones were found in a chest in the Tower in 1674 and buried in Westminster Abbey, but without DNA testing, no proof exists that they are those of the princes.

Above: Richard III was blamed for the murder of the two young princes, and Shakespeare portrayed him as a villain. Recent historical works suggest things weren't quite so black and white.

AT A GLANCE

SOME HISTORIANS CLAIM THE YOUNG PRINCES IN THE TOWER WERE GIVEN NEW IDENTITIES, PROTECTED BY HENRY VII AND ELIZABETH WOODVILLE. ONE VERSION SUGGESTS THAT EDWARD V DIED OF NATURAL CAUSES, WHILE RICHARD LIVED IN OBSCURITY AS A BRICKLAYER IN ESSEX. MORE CERTAIN IS THAT THE TUDORS FOUGHT OFF "PRETENDERS," THE MOST THREATENING BEING PERKIN WARBECK, A FLEMISH JACK-THE-LAD WHO CLAIMED HE WAS PRINCE RICHARD. AFTER TRYING TO ESCAPE FROM THE TOWER, HE WAS HANGED IN 1499.

Above: William Rufus lies dead in the New Forest.
Walter Tirel is seen here riding away, but whether he is a
murderer fleeing or a subject riding to fetch help after a
tragic accident is not known.

HEADS ON THE BLOCK

The Tower of London has been the last earthly abode for many prisoners doomed to die on the block by the sword or the ax.

Henry VIII's reign saw a steady flow of noble prisoners into the Tower, often through the river entrance known then as the watergate, but today known as Traitors' Gate. Thomas More was beheaded on Tower Hill in 1535 for refusing to acknowledge the King as head of the English Church. Within a year, Henry's second wife, the bewitching Anne Boleyn, had also been beheaded—executed at her request by a French swordsman. Her "crime" was betraying the King by her adultery, supposedly with five men, who were all executed, too. Evidence hardly counted in the face of Henry's rage and frustration at Anne's failure to give him a healthy son (she had only borne him a daughter, the future Queen Elizabeth I). Yet Anne was almost certainly innocent, at least of adultery with the men named at the times and places set out in her indictment.

In 1542, Catherine Howard, fifth wife of Henry VIII, was also beheaded for adultery. Beside her died Jane Boleyn, Lady Rochford, her "accomplice." Henry VIII's court was riven by feuds between the Seymours (the brothers of his third wife, Jane Seymour) and the Howards. Another Howard, the Earl of Surrey, was executed in 1547, when Henry became convinced that Howard had planned to usurp the crown from his son, the future Edward VI.

Thomas Seymour was executed in 1549, his brother Edward in 1552. When sickly Edward VI died in 1553, the Duke of Northumberland tried to make his daughter-in-law Lady Jane Grey queen, usurping Henry's daughters, the princesses Mary and Elizabeth. After nine days, Mary's supporters won the power-struggle and 14-year-old Lady Jane, an innocent, was told by her father Suffolk she was no longer queen. In February 1554, she and her husband were executed. Suffolk and Northumberland soon followed them to the block.

Top: Anne Boleyn, second wife of King Henry VIII. She was executed in 1536 for treason, including adultery. She asked to be beheaded by a swordsman.

Left: The executioner's ax did not always sever a head with one blow. The execution of Lady Salisbury in 1541 reportedly needed 11 blows.

Above: A coin (a half-groat) from the reign of Henry VIII. The condemned usually paid their executioner out of their own pocket, as well as forgiving him in advance for his actions.

Above: Lady Jane Grey blindfolded before the block. Made queen by her scheming father-in-law, the blameless Jane was beheaded on 12th February, 1554, after being the "uncrowned" queen of England for nine days.

Above: Prisoners who entered the Tower by the watergate seldom came out alive. One who did was Anne Boleyn's daughter, Elizabeth, in the reign of her half-sister Mary I.

AT A GLANCE

ELIZABETH I, AS A 21-YEAR-OLD PRINCESS, PASSED THROUGH TRAITORS' GATE IN 1554, FEARFUL OF THE SAME FATE AS HER MOTHER ANNE BOLEYN. SHE WAS SUSPECTED OF CONSPIRING WITH SIR THOMAS WYATT AGAINST QUEEN MARY I (HER HALF-SISTER). WYATT SWORE SHE WAS INNOCENT, BEFORE HE WAS BEHEADED AND ELIZABETH WAS RELEASED FROM THE TOWER.

TRAGIC MARY

Mary Stuart, Queen of Scots, was a romantic but tragic figure. A prisoner in exile for 18 years, she died on the block in 1587.

Just before her execution, Mary remarked to an attendant, "Did I not tell you this would happen? I knew they would never allow me to you live. . ." She believed her Catholic faith caused her downfall, though politics as much as religion caused Mary's head to roll.

Mary became Queen of Scotland in 1542, as a baby, after her father James V died broken-hearted at defeat by the English. Mary was raised in France and married the heir to the French throne, becoming Queen of France in 1559. But when her husband Francis died the following year, she returned to Scotland, a land she barely knew, with its prating Protestant clerics and feuding nobles. In 1565, Mary married her cousin, Lord Darnley, a Catholic who was related to the royal Tudors. By 1566 she was pregnant, but already out of love, for in a vicious act of jealousy and rage, Darnley had had her secretary, David Rizzio, stabbed to death. By the time Mary gave birth to her son James in June 1566, she may already have found a new love in James Hepburn, Earl of Bothwell.

Then, on the night of February 10, 1567, a sensational murder enveloped Mary in scandal. A house in Edinburgh was blown up by gunpowder, the blast waking Mary in Holyrood House. Her husband Darnley was found dead in the garden, strangled. On May 15, Mary married Bothwell. Her reputation was in tatters. Had she conspired to murder Darnley? Was she a willing bride or a woman "ravished" by a brutal abductor? The Scots nobles turned against her and forced her to abdicate in favor of her son.

Above: Queen Elizabeth I of England and Mary shared a royal ancestor: King Henry VII, founder of the Tudor line. He was Elizabeth's grandfather and Mary's great-grandfather.

Below: Holyrood House in Edinburgh is where Mary's secretary Rizzio was murdered. Queen Victoria asked to see the murder-room on her first visit in 1850 and was shown bloodstains on the floor.

AT A GLANCE

MARY'S CLAIM TO THE ENGLISH THRONE WAS THROUGH HER GRANDMOTHER, MARGARET TUDOR, SISTER OF HENRY VIII. MARY SUCCEEDED HER FATHER JAMES V IN SCOTLAND, IN 1542. HENRY DIED IN 1547. AFTER HENRY CAME HIS SON EDWARD VI, HIS ELDER DAUGHTER MARY I AND THEN ELIZABETH I IN 1558. SO LONG AS ELIZABETH REMAINED CHILDLESS, MARY WAS NEXT IN LINE, BUT IN THE END, HER SON JAMES TOOK HER PLACE IN BOTH SCOTLAND AND ENGLAND.

Above: Mary Stuart, Queen of Scots. When she left France for her
native Scotland, she was plunged into a world of conspiracy, jealousy
and religious fanaticism.

Above: The death of David Rizzio, Italian secretary and card-partner of Mary Queen of Scots. Mary's husband Darnley planned and supervised the brutal slaying by multiple stab wounds.

Mary then fled to England, where her cousin Queen Elizabeth I, ambivalent as always, kept her a prisoner for 18 years. Elizabeth was unwilling to send Mary back to possible death in Scotland at the hands of her enemies, but was also fearful of Catholic-inspired plots in England, encouraged by France or Spain. It suited her and her government, to have the infant James on the throne of Scotland rather than the potentially meddlesome Mary. In 1570, fears of plots were increased when the Pope excommunicated Elizabeth (outlawing her from the Catholic Church) and sanctioned her removal.

EVIDENCE

AFTER DARNLEY'S MURDER, MARY WAS LAMPOONED IN SCOTTISH SCANDAL-SHEETS AS A WHORE. FEW PEOPLE BELIEVED THE "ABDUCTION" STORY, DECIDING THAT SHE HAD RUN OFF WILLINGLY WITH BOTHWELL, WHO LATER DESERTED HER.

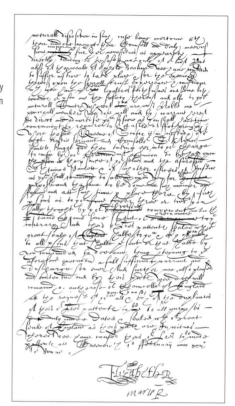

Right: The signed document from England's Privy Council ordering the execution of Mary Queen of Scots after her trial in October 1586. Her son James made no move or appeal to save her life.

Left: Queen Elizabeth confers with her spymaster, Sir Francis Walsingham. His agents and informers trapped Mary into her fatal involvement in the Babington Plot, a conspiracy that Walsingham covertly managed.

In the middle of the web of intrigue sat Elizabeth's spymaster, Sir Francis Walsingham, whose agents set up a cipher code system to monitor a fatal plot, exposed in 1586. Antony Babington led a hot-headed Catholic conspiracy to kill Elizabeth, bring in foreign soldiers and make Mary queen. Letters between Mary and the Babington plotters went straight to Walsingham, sealing Mary's fate. Elizabeth signed the death warrant (afterward denying she'd done so) and Mary was executed on February 8, 1587. The executioner needed two blows to sever Mary's head, which caused her wig to fall off. Her clothes were burned, to leave no relics.

Above: Mary was executed at Fotheringay Castle. Her remains were interred at Peterborough Cathedral, but she was exhumed in 1612 at the orders of her son James I, and reburied in Westminster Abbey.

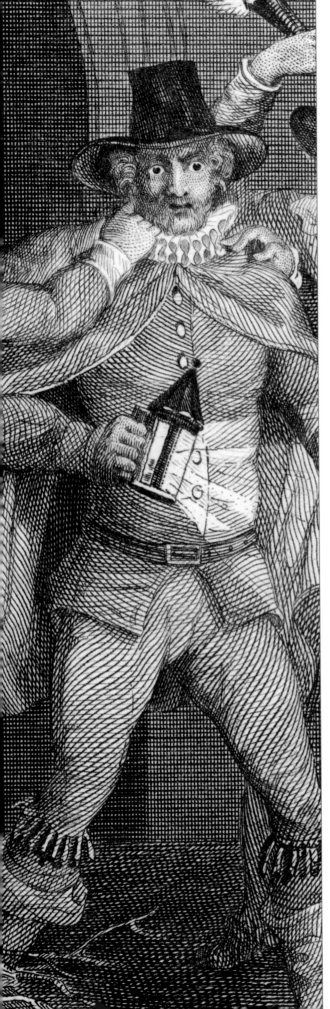

THE GUNPOWDER PLOT

Guy Fawkes tried to blow up the Houses of Parliament—as most people know, but behind the familiar story lies an unsolved mystery.

Guy Fawkes, born in York in 1570, was a Catholic in a Protestant kingdom. English Catholics hoped that James I, who succeeded Elizabeth I in 1603, would do away with some of the many laws that discriminated against Catholics. When these hopes were dashed, Fawkes joined a conspiracy led by Robert Catesby. The conspirators' radical plan involved blowing up the Houses of Parliament, killing or scaring away the king and putting his daughter Elizabeth on the throne with a Catholic husband.

By late 1605 there were 13 conspirators. The chosen "bomber" was Guy Fawkes, who knew something about gunpowder from his days as a soldier. Using the name John Johnson, he took a rented house close to the Palace of Westminster and stacked its cellar with 36 barrels of gunpowder, rowed across the Thames from Catesby's house in Lambeth. On the evening of November 4, 1605, Fawkes hid in the cellar and waited.

EVIDENCE?

AFTER HIS ARREST, FAWKES KEPT SILENT FOR TWO DAYS, BUT RACKED IN AGONY UNDER TORTURE HE FINALLY GASPED OUT THE NAMES OF THE OTHER CONSPIRATORS. CATESBY AND THE OTHERS HAD FLED LONDON AND ENDED UP AT HOLBEACH HOUSE IN THE MIDLANDS, WHERE THEY WERE TRAPPED BY 200 SOLDIERS. TRYING TO DRY OUT DAMP GUNPOWDER, THEY CAUSED AN EXPLOSIVE FIRE THAT BLINDED ONE OF THEM. IN THE FIGHT THAT FOLLOWED, CATESBY AND A FEW OF THE OTHERS WERE KILLED. THE REST WERE DRAGGED AWAY FOR TRIAL AND EXECUTION AT THE GALLOWS.

Left: Guy Fawkes was discovered under the House of Lords. The first searchers mistook him for a servant.

Above: Following torture on the rack, Guy Fawkes eventually revealed the names of his fellow-conspirators. This is his statement, made under duress, the signature that of a broken man. He went to the gallows in January 1606.

What Fawkes didn't know was that the plotters had already been betrayed. On October 26, Lord Monteagle received an anonymous letter warning him to stay away from Parliament on November 5. Monteagle took the letter to Robert Cecil, chief minister, and Cecil told King James. The king ordered a search of Parliament and the surrounding buildings. At first the searchers ignored a "tall man" beside a stack of firewood (a servant, perhaps). But about midnight, a second search party arrested "a very tall and desperate fellow," who was Guy Fawkes. Catesby and the others fled. Some were killed resisting arrest and the others, including Fawkes, were hanged.

The plot was more bad news for Catholics and who wrote the letter to Lord Monteagle remains a mystery.

THE DISAPPEARING PRINCE

In 1789, revolution threw France into turmoil. Four years later the French king and his queen were dead. So what happened to their son?

Louis XVI or Louis Bourbon as his republican captors called him, was a victim of the Reign of Terror, the bloodiest period of France's revolution. The guillotine was busy despatching dozens of reviled aristocrats, blamed by radicals for all France's ills under the old regime. King Louis went to the guillotine in 1793, followed a few months later by Marie-Antoinette.

The royal couple had two surviving children (their eldest son died in 1789); a daughter and a son, the Dauphin Louis-Charles, born in 1785. He was 8 years old when his parents were executed and was given into the care first of a cobbler and then, it's said, of a married couple of gaolers while revolutionary leaders considered his fate. The noble-born revolutionary Barras visited "a boy" in prison in the summer of 1794 and found not the healthy prince, but a child dying of consumption (tuberculosis).

Was this the Dauphin or an impostor? Years later, the gaoler's wife said she and her husband had smuggled the prince out of prison, substituting a lookalike boy who was dying anyway.

Above: A 19th-century engraving of Louis-Charles, the disappearing prince, from a painting made of him in 1792, when he was 7 years old.

Below: Marie-Antoinette says a tearful farewell to her son. The king was guillotined in January 1793 and the queen was kept in solitary confinement until she, too, was executed in October 1793, not knowing her son's fate.

Some officials were sure the dying boy was not the prince. Nevertheless the Dauphin Louis-Charles's death was announced in 1795; whereupon a banker named Petival declared the death certificate to be a forgery. Petival and his family were murdered soon afterward. An odd reference by Barras to "the child you know" being unharmed by this crime suggests he knew Petival had the prince in his care.

Years later, in 1846 and again in 1894, the coffin of the dead prince was opened and doctors agreed that the bones were those of a teenager aged 15 or 16, not a boy of 10. So what did happen to the Bourbon prince, now in royalist eyes the king of France? When the Bourbon monarchy was restored in 1815, 27 people claimed to be the lost Louis-Charles. One contender, named Karl Wilhelm Naundorff, in 1833, seemed plausible, but Naundorff was shunned by the princess, his "sister," who had survived the Revolution. Naundorff left France fearing arrest or worse and died in Holland, still claiming to be France's rightful king.

Below: Marie Antoinette's trial began in October 1793, ten months after the execution of her husband. It lasted two days and she was convicted of high treason.

Inset: Statues of King Louis XVI and Marie-Antoinette, parents of the lost prince of France, in Saint-Denis Cathedral, Paris.

Above: Rasputin in 1908. According to rumors, his alleged influence over the tsar's wife extended to her bed. Prince Felix may have used his wife as bait to trap Rasputin, enticing him to the palace with the hint of an orgy.

RASPUTIN AND THE ROMANOVS

**What was Rasputin's secret hold over Russia's Empress?
And what really happened to the Tsar's family in 1918?**

Grigori Rasputin was a Russian peasant-priest and mystic – wild-eyed, long-haired, filthy, yet able to heal the sick and bewitch high society in St Petersburg. Venerated as divinely inspired, Rasputin also had an irresistible sexual technique: he told fashionable ladies they must sin with him to gain salvation.

The Tsarina Alexandra believed Rasputin could cure her hemophiliac son Alexei and allowed the priest familiar access to the court and family from 1905. However, as Rasputin's debauched behavior became more scandalous and his influence more dangerous, a group of courtiers and ministers plotted to kill him. In December 1916, they first gave Rasputin poison and then shot him. Rasputin, however, clung on to life and only eventually died when he was pushed through a hole in the ice in the River Neva, where he drowned.

Rasputin's death could not save the Russian Empire. Revolution and Russia's near-total collapse in 1917 during the First World War, brought down the Romanov dynasty. After Lenin and the Bolsheviks took power, Tsar Nicholas II was forced to abdicate. What would happen to him and his family? Exile seemed likely, perhaps in Britain, whose King George V was the Tsar's cousin. But there was no rescue. The Tsar and Tsarina, with their five children (Alexei, Olga, Maria, Tatiana and Anastasia) were held prisoner, first outside St Petersburg and then at Ekaterinburg in the Ural Mountains. There, on July 19, 1918, they were taken to a cellar and shot. So were their doctor and three servants. The bodies were burnt and thrown down a mine-shaft.

Above: Russia's imperial family: Tsar Nicholas II with the Tsarina Alexandra and their five children (from left to right): Maria (b. 1899), Alexei (b. 1904), Olga (b. 1895), Tatiana (b. 1897) and Anastasia (b. 1901).

EVIDENCE?

AFTER THE DEATHS OF THE ROMANOV GIRLS, AT LEAST 10 WOMEN CLAIMED TO BE THE GRAND DUCHESS ANASTASIA. THE MOST PERSISTENT "PRETENDER" WAS ANNA ANDERSON, WHO OFFERED SOME "RECOLLECTIONS" OF ROYAL FAMILY LIFE AND HAD A SLIGHT PHYSICAL RESEMBLANCE (BUNIONS AND SCARS). HOWEVER, DNA TESTS AFTER HER DEATH IN 1984 DISPROVED ANY GENETIC TIE TO THE ROMANOVS. GRAND DUKE CYRIL, THE TSAR'S COUSIN, REFUSED TO SEE HER AND A FORMER ROYAL TUTOR SAID HER RUSSIAN WAS SO POOR SHE COULD NOT POSSIBLY BE THE REAL ANASTASIA.

Left: The Yusupov Palace in St Petersburg, where Prince Felix Yusupov and his fellow conspirators lured Rasputin to a violent death in 1916.

Above: Mandy Rice-Davies, the blonde in the Keeler-Profumo affair. Her remark made in court "Well he would, wouldn't he?" (in response to a witness denying he'd ever met her) passed into journalistic folklore.

SEX IN HIGH PLACES

The Profumo affair had sex, lies and spies, all in one heady cocktail. A government minister became the centre of a scandal involving prostitutes, parties and nuclear secrets.

The story began in 1960 when 18-year-old Christine Keeler got a job in a Soho club. After meeting Stephen Ward, an osteopath with connections, Keeler and her blonde friend Mandy Rice-Davies became on-call party girls. In July 1961, at a party at Cliveden, the Astors' estate, Keeler cavorting nude in the swimming pool, caught the eye of war minister John Profumo. High profile and married to actress Valerie Hobson, Profumo embarked on a fling with Keeler.

Keeler was generous with her favours. At the same time as she was going to bed with Profumo, she was seeing Yevgeni (Eugene) Ivanov, Soviet naval attaché and spy. It's unlikely that Profumo chatted in bed about military secrets with Keeler, a girl more interested in a good time than in nuclear payloads, but after MI5 got wind and issued a quiet warning, Profumo quickly ended the affair. By now whispers were circulating about "a minister and a call-girl."

EVIDENCE?

STEPHEN WARD'S DEATH WHILE ON TRIAL WAS RULED TO BE SUICIDE. BUT SOME PEOPLE SPECULATED AT THE TIME THAT THE SECURITY SERVICES HAD "ELIMINATED" HIM, TO PREVENT MORE REVELATIONS ABOUT SEX PARTIES AND PROMINENT PEOPLE. IVANOV WENT BACK TO MOSCOW, HIS WIFE LEFT HIM AND HE DIED IN 1994. JOHN PROFUMO REDEEMED HIS REPUTATION BY YEARS OF CHARITY WORK, HIS WIFE VALERIE HOBSON STUCK BY HIM AND HE DIED IN 2006.

Above: Christine Keeler, the center of media attention outside London's Marylebone magistrates' court in 1963 during the trial that rocked the Macmillan government.

In 1962, Keeler's lover Aloysius "lucky" Gordon stabbed another of her lovers, Johnny Edgecombe. The case of the good-time girl with drug-dealer boyfriends led to open press interest and rumours about her involvement with a government minister. In March 1963, after allegations voiced in the House of Commons (protected by MPs' privilege), Profumo denied any impropriety. But the cat was now out of the bag and in June, the War Minister resigned, admitting that he had lied about his relationship with Keeler.

MI5 interviewed Christine Keeler and, while judging her no Mata Hari, decided there was at least a chance that Ivanov, using Stephen Ward as a go-between, could have used Keeler as a "honey-trap" to wheedle secrets from Profumo. Ward was arrested and charged with living on money from prostitution; in August he was found dead at home, from an overdose of sleeping pills. The report on the Profumo affair came out in September and in October prime minister Harold Macmillan resigned, on health grounds. Keeler was jailed for nine months for perjury, while the Conservative government staggered on into 1964, when Labour easily won the general election.

Top: Monica Lewinsky in 1999. President Clinton's "was it sex or wasn't it?" liaison with the young intern earned her fleeting notoriety. This is another example of a scandalous affair in office.

Left: Cliveden, home of the Astors from 1893. It was here that John Profumo saw Christine Keeler at a pool party that became notorious.

LORD ON THE RUN

The "case of the vanishing peer" hit the headlines in 1974. Did Lord Lucan conspire with a hitman to have his wife murdered, only for things to go horribly wrong? Or did he get away with murder himself?

Richard John Bingham, 7th Earl of Lucan (born 1934) was an establishment man: Eton, Coldstream Guards, city bank, lucky at cards, with a wife and three children, and a house Belgravia. By 1974, however, "lucky" Lucan had run out of luck. He had money problems, and he and his wife were estranged and battling over their three children. He told friends Lady Lucan was going mad.

Between 8:30 and 9:00 pm on Thursday November 7, 1974, the Lucans' nanny Sandra Rivett, having put the two younger children to bed, went down to make a pot of tea. Upstairs at 46 Lower Belgrave Street, Lady Lucan was watching TV. Lord Lucan was at his flat or his club. Downstairs, Sandra Rivett was battered to death. At 9:15 pm, Lady Lucan went to see what had happened to the tea, whereupon (she told police) she was attacked by her husband, but fought him off. With blood on his clothes, Lucan confessed to killing Sandra by mistake.

At 9:45 pm, Lady Lucan, injured and bloodstained, fled to the Plumber's Arms. The police discovered the body and a length of lead pipe, but Lucan had gone.

Lucan's story was that he had disturbed an intruder assaulting his wife, but fearing she would accuse him, he had fled. His friends reckoned that he had drowned himself by scuttling his boat in the English Channel, remorseful that he had killed the wrong woman. Another theory was that Lucan had hired a hitman to kill his wife and that when he found the wrong body in the sack, Lucan then attacked his wife himself. At the inquest, Lucan was named as the murderer. In 1999, the High Court declared the vanishing peer officially "deceased" in legal terms.

However, unconfirmed sightings of Lucan have continued, and private investigations have continued both to prove Lucan's death and to prove he's still alive. Over forty years later, Lucan is occasionally still making headlines.

Above: Lady Lucan on the day of her marriage to Lucan. Whether she was the intended murder victim will never be known.

THE TRUTH?

RUMORS PERSISTED THAT FRIENDS HAD SMUGGLED LUCAN OUT OF THE COUNTRY TO BEGIN A NEW LIFE IN AFRICA. THEN, IN A 2012 TV DOCUMENTARY, A PERSONAL ASSISTANT OF LUCAN'S CLOSE FRIEND JOHN ASPINALL SAID THAT ON ASPINALL'S INSTRUCTIONS, SHE HAD ARRANGED FOR LUCAN'S TWO ELDEST CHILDREN TO VISIT AFRICA BETWEEN 1979 AND 1981, SO THAT THEIR FATHER COULD SEE HOW THEY WERE GROWING UP WITHOUT MAKING CONTACT WITH THEM. LADY LUCAN DENIED THAT THE CHILDREN HAD BEEN TO AFRICA AT THAT TIME.

A SELECTION OF SIGHTINGS AND NEWS STORIES

- 1974: A man believed to be Lucan was arrested by Australian police, but it proved to be John Stonehouse, a Labour MP who had faked his own death just one month previously.

- 2003: A former Scotland Yard detective claimed to have found Lucan, living as an aging hippy in Goa, India. It later transpired that the man was Barry Halpin, or Jungly Barry, a well-known musician.

- 2004: Scotland Yard reopened the case, but the fresh hunt gave no results.

- 2007: Residents in Marton, New Zealand, claimed that Lucan was living in a broken-down Land Rover with a cat, a goat, and a possum. The man in question identified as Roger Woodgate and claimed to be 10 years younger than Lucan.

- 2016: An associate of Lucan's claimed that the peer had shot himself, and that his body had been fed to a tiger in a private zoo owned by one of his friends.

- 2016: After several attempts, Lord Lucan's son obtained a death certificate for his father, allowing him to inherit Lord Lucan's titles and estate.

Above: Outside the Lucan home in London's fashionable Belgravia, Lady Lucan was watching TV at the time of the murder.

Right: At the inquest into the death of Sandra Rivett, "Lucky Lucan" was named as her murderer. After his disappearance, reports that he was still alive never went away.

LORD LUCAN DID FLEE TO AFRICA

WORLD EXCLUSIVE

By STEVE MYALL and MARTIN FRICKER

LORD Lucan fled to Africa and could still be alive, his brother has sensationally told the Mirror.

Hugh Bingham, 72, said the missing earl, who would now be 76, escaped to begin a new life after murdering his children's nanny 36 years ago.

Breaking his silence for the first time, he said he's "sure" Lucan went to Africa and may still be hiding there.

FULL STORY: PAGES 2,3,4&5

111

DEATH OF DIANA

Diana, Princess of Wales, died on August 31, 1997, in a car crash in Paris. Her death became a cause célèbre. Was it an accident or the result of a high-level conspiracy, as many of Diana's devotees wanted to believe?

The official cause of the accident was high speed and heavy drinking by the driver, Henri Paul. Skeptics claimed Paul was not drunk; he was either framed or was working for MI6. The involvement of the British secret service was alleged by former MI6 agent Richard Tomlinson, who claimed Diana was bugged and followed. Had a white Fiat Uno, never traced, collided with the Mercedes? This seems an unlikely method for murder. Did spooks flash lights into the driver's eyes? Absurd, according to experts. The victims, Diana and her boyfriend Dodi Fayed, were not wearing seat belts. Had their belts been tampered with? In 2006, a police inquiry (Operation Paget) was opened into the conspiracies surrounding Diana's death. It found that any surveillance had been routine.

At the inquest, details emerged of a letter that Diana had written to her butler: "This part of my life is the most dangerous," she wrote. She went on to say that her husband, Prince Charles, was planning "an accident" in her car, so that he could remarry. A close friend of Diana, Lucia Flecha de Lima, dismissed the letter as a possible forgery. Operation Paget found no evidence of a conspiracy and concluded that Diana's death was the result of a tragic accident.

Below: Diana was an international media target, a victim of the celebrity she had often welcomed after her marriage breakup.

Below: The entrance to the road tunnel into which the Mercedes car accelerated at high speed, pursued by photographers.

Below: A wall at Pont D'Alma has been inscribed with messages to Diana, and people leave flowers for her.

AT A GLANCE

DIANA AND DODI FAYED LEFT THE RITZ HOTEL AT 12:20 AM. DRIVER HENRI PAUL DROVE OFF AT OVER TWICE THE SPEED LIMIT, TO ELUDE PHOTOGRAPHERS. AT 12:23 AM, THE CAR CRASHED. FAYED AND PAUL WERE KILLED OUTRIGHT. DIANA DIED LATER IN HOSPITAL. SECURITY MAN TREVOR REES-JONES SURVIVED, BUT WAS BADLY INJURED.

Below: The Ritz hotel, Paris. Here Diana and Dodi Fayed ate dinner before the fateful dash from the hotel.

Above: Mohamed Al-Fayed, Dodi's father, claimed Diana and Dodi were engaged and that Diana was pregnant—claims rejected by friends and medical evidence.

Above: Prince Philip, Charles' father and Diana's ex-father-in-law. The inquest dismissed suggestions that he or any member of the British royal family was involved in Diana's death.

Ritz Hotel

Site of Accident

Above: This is the route through central Paris taken by the Mercedes and the pursuing paparazzi.

FAMOUS FACES

When we are drawn to people, it's usually for a strong reason. As more and more people are drawn to person, the bigger and bigger a reaction will be to what the person does or what happens to them. So, when questions involve someone with celebrity status, it's little wonder that theories spread about their fate.

The truth about the likes of Hollywood is often tawdry, at times glaringly lit, at times shadowed by the publicity machinery. Stars of film, stage, music, television and social influence live their lives in public. Celebrities feed off the media, but they can also be devoured by it. Hollywood, in its heyday, was a cauldron of conspiracies; studio bosses plotting to steal each other's stars, the stars themselves hiding private lives and loves. While gossip columns and websites churn out stories of stars pepped by pills, drink and drugs, of sexual scandals and personal tragedies, all the while critics argue that the entertainment industry has itself become a conspiracy—to manipulate our emotions (as art does) and to shape ideas and attitudes.

Above: Early horror movies created fantasies about aliens and oversized dinosaurs that played on the American audience's fears of Communist threats and nuclear war.

HOLLYWOOD INFLUENCE

Good or bad, movies certainly influence us and movie stars become role models. Is this just how art works, or do moviemakers set out to deliberately change our perceptions and attitudes—not always for the best?

Conspiracy theorists argue that ever since the first movies flickered on screen in the early 1900s, some moviemakers have used their huge power at the behest of their paymasters. Science fiction films of the 1950s were made to downplay the existence of real UFOs and aliens and/or to harden attitudes toward the Soviet Union and China. Some claim that "Mob-money" shapes movie output, that Disney's *Fantasia* is full of references to Illuminati black magic, that Errol Flynn was a Nazi sympathizer (in fact he was inclined to the left), that the CIA killed James Dean because he was a leader of teenage rebellion and, famously, that Stanley Kubrick directed the Apollo Moon landings. Certainly moviemaking is seldom free of intrigue and a fair bit of double-dealing, and the line between art and propaganda can be thin. Around the world, moviemakers are routinely used by governments for propaganda, as pioneered by Nazi lies-spinner Josef Goebbels in the 1930s.

Below: Science fiction movies offer vehicles for environmental or political messages—and may encourage some people to think that aliens from outer space are already here!

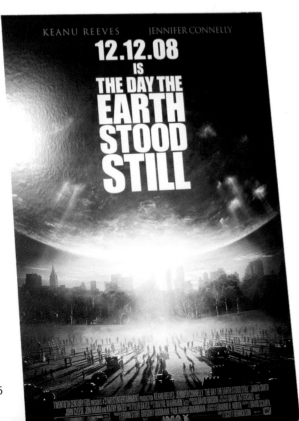

AT A GLANCE

HOLLYWOOD HAS CASHED IN ON AND FED THE PUBLIC APPETITE FOR CONSPIRACY THROUGH A STRING OF HIT MOVIES OVER THE YEARS. EXAMPLES ARE *JFK* (THE KENNEDY KILLING); *ALL THE PRESIDENT'S MEN* (WATERGATE); *THE BOYS FROM BRAZIL* (NAZIS HIDING AWAY IN SOUTH AMERICA); *THE DAY OF THE JACKAL* (THE PLOT TO ASSASSINATE FRENCH LEADER CHARLES DE GAULLE) AND THE *BOURNE* FILMS (DON'T TRUST ANYONE!).

The SPECTRE organization in the Bond films is, according to some conspiracy theorists, none other than the Illuminati—who some say control the movie industry. Cinema mirrors shifts in popular concerns: from Cold War fears, when horror films portrayed hometown America menaced by aliens, giant spiders and jellylike blobs, through to today's preoccupation with terrorist plots, environmental threats, corruption and conspiracy in government.

Top: At a time of anti-Red paranoia, Superman and other comic book superheroes came to represent the American ideal of battling evil. They went on to spawn billion-dollar movie blockbusters.

Right: Daniel Craig was the 6th screen James Bond. Bond moves through a turbulent world in which Britain, through 007 and M, is still at the heart of the action.

AMELIA EARHART

Amelia Earhart was the most famous woman pilot of the 1930s. Her disappearance in 1937 sparked an unsuccessful search of the Pacific and left in its wake an ongoing mystery.

Enthusiasts for conspiracies suggest that Earhart's disappearance was more than just a flying accident. With navigator Fred Noonan, she took off from California on May 20, 1937. By July 1, they were in New Guinea, having flown 32,000 km (20,000 miles) in stages. The next day, Earhart radioed that the plane was low on fuel. Nothing more was seen or heard of her.

Earhart's disappearance spawned conspiracy ideas. One theory is that she was asked to spy on Japanese naval activity (although the U.S. did not go to war with Japan until 1941) and was shot down and either died or was taken prisoner. Some think she died in a Japanese jail, others that she was freed in 1945 and given a new identity as businesswoman Irene Bolam, until her death in 1982. Or, did she fake her own disappearance, perhaps to elope with Noonan? Her husband, U.S. publisher George Putnam, had her declared legally dead in 1939. The most way-out fantasy is that Amelia Earhart was abducted by aliens—a storyline that found its way into a 1995 *Star Trek: Voyager* episode on TV.

THE EVIDENCE?

IT SEEMS MOST LIKELY THAT EARHART AND NOONAN DIED AS CASTAWAYS. AIR PHOTOS TAKEN IN 1938 MAY SHOW FOOTPRINTS, AND IN 1940, THE BRITISH DISCOVERED HUMAN BONES ON NIKUMARORO. OTHER ARTIFACTS FOUND INCLUDE A MIRROR, A KNIFE AND U.S.-MADE BOTTLES. DNA EVIDENCE COULD SOLVE THE MYSTERY OF EARHART'S FINAL FLIGHT ONCE AND FOR ALL.

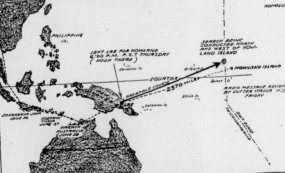

NEW PHOTO DISCOVERY REIGNITES CONSPIRACY THEORIES

When retired U.S. treasury agent Les Kinney came across a photo taken in the 1930s, he thought he had found the answer to the mystery of Earhart's disappearance. The image, taken on the Japanese-occupied Marshall Islands, appeared to show Earhart and Noonan on a wharf in 1937. In the photo, discovered in the U.S. national archives, a woman with short hair is sitting with her back toward the camera. A figure resembling Noonan can also be seen.

Experts agreed, and the History Channel promptly produced a documentary that drew heavily on the "new evidence," which seemed to prove the theory that Earhart died in Japanese custody after being taken prisoner. Facial recognition technology seemed to show that the two figures in question were very likely to be Earhart and Noonan.

However, not everyone was convinced. A Tokyo-based blogger, Kota Yamano, claimed to have discovered that the photo had actually been published in 1935—two years before Earhart's disappearance. Other experts have also cast doubt on the claims.

Right: Amelia Earhart (seen here in 1936) was the first woman to fly the Atlantic solo (1932). She was already a celebrity before her 1937 disappearance.

Left: Faint SOS signals were heard following her disappearance in the area she was last seen, but she was never found.

HOW DID MARILYN DIE?

On the night of August 4, 1962, the world's most famous movie star died. Was Marilyn Monroe's death an accident, suicide. . . or murder?

The Los Angeles coroner's verdict was "probably suicide," resulting from a drug overdose. Aged only 36, Marilyn had come a long way from Norma Jean Baker, starlet and pin-up. Marilyn Monroe radiated superstar brilliance on and off the screen. Her private life was complicated, her marriages to baseball hero Joe Di Maggio and playwright Arthur Miller front-page news. Secret lovers included President John F. Kennedy.

Off-screen, Monroe was deeply insecure, unable to sleep without pills, addicted to barbiturates and heavily reliant on psychoanalysis. Suicide or accidental overdose seemed feasible causes for her death, but fans, theorists and some Monroe biographers conjured scenarios in which she was killed by a barbiturates enema that reacted fatally with the cocktail of other medication. The most lurid version has Mafia hit-men forcibly administering the rectal dose.

Monroe's frailty and potential for indiscretion was, it's claimed, a threat to the Kennedys. Both John and Bobby had reportedly been Marilyn's lovers, while hovering in the shadows was Mafia boss Sam Giancana. One version of her death blames agents, either working for the Kennedys (to eliminate Marilyn as a danger) or paid by the Mafia or the CIA to enmesh the Kennedys in a murder and so wreck their political careers. It was hard for Monroe's millions of fans to accept that this icon of glamour, albeit often a tragic figure, could have played her last scene face-down on a bed in her bungalow with a bottle of sleeping pills on the bedside table. More comforting surely to imagine her as innocent victim, used, abused and finally discarded by the powerful men she had beguiled, but for whom she had become a liability.

Above: A birth certificate said to be Monroe's. Her birth-name was either Norma Jean Baker or Norma Jean (or Jeane) Mortenson, born in Los Angeles.

Below: A 1954 magazine cover. Marilyn, then 28, had just emerged from bit-parts to starring roles in hits such as *Gentlemen Prefer Blondes* (1953).

Right: Marilyn Monroe's star on Hollywood's Walk of Fame. Her beauty, life and death made her one of the most written-about movie stars of all time.

Above: A typical Monroe publicity photo—the sex-goddess of 1950s Hollywood. She made 28 films in a career that began in 1948 with the film Dangerous Years—an ominous title perhaps.

EVIDENCE?

HUNDREDS OF BOOKS HAVE BEEN WRITTEN ABOUT MARILYN MONROE, SOME WITH TALES OF "SECRET TAPES" AND "PRIVATE DIARIES" CLAIMING TO REVEAL THE HIDDEN TRUTH. THE MORE LIKELY REALITY IS THAT HER DEATH WAS A TRAGIC ACCIDENT. SHE WENT TO BED AT 8:00 PM, HAVING AT 5:15 PM CALLED HER DOCTOR RALPH GREENSON ABOUT HER SLEEPING PROBLEM. AT 3:00 AM, EUNICE MURRAY, HER HOUSEKEEPER, SEEING THE LIGHT STILL ON, FOUND THE BODY.

ELVIS LIVES!

Fans often cannot accept that their rock idols are mortal, so they come up with strange theories to explain their sudden passing.

The untimely death, at the age of 42, of Elvis Aaron Presley on August 16, 1977, seemed sadly inevitable. "The King" of rock 'n' roll had become a caricature of his former self, bloated by ill-health, drug abuse and over-eating. His death from a drugs overdose (largely antidepressants and sleeping pills) was widely mourned by his fans and his place in the pop pantheon assured.

Among his many fans were some who simply denied that Elvis was dead, despite the fact that after his death, his body had lain in an open casket at Graceland for his fans to file past. "No, Elvis lives!" was the cry and reports of Elvis sightings continued for years. Conspiracists claim he was a secret agent working for the FBI and U.S. anti-narcotics agencies, his "death" faked to protect him from vengeance-seeking drug cartels and give him a new identity.

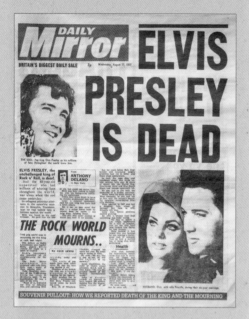

Above: Newspapers were filled with news of Elvis's death. He was loved around the world, both for his music and his films.

Above: Elvis the King in full swing, on tour in April 1972 — no longer the slim youth of the 1950s, but still rocking.

Rumors have followed the deaths of other pop heroes, too: Brian Jones of The Rolling Stones (dead in a swimming pool), Jim Morrison of The Doors (drug overdose, murder, not dead at all?), Jimi Hendrix (choked on vomit, suicide, murder?) and Michael Jackson (drugs, but how induced?).

How John Lennon died seemed more clear. In 1980, the former Beatle, aged 40, was shot in New York City by Mark Chapman, a deranged fan who had earlier been given Lennon's autograph. Fellow-Beatle George Harrison survived a knife attack in 1999, fighting off his assailant with a poker, but died from cancer in 2001. Paul McCartney was rumored to have "died" in 1966, in a car accident and been replaced by a double. Was there a clue in the song Revolution 9? Played backward, some people claim the sound of a car crash can be heard and the words "turn me on, dead man." Paul went on performing, however and most people give no more than a second's consideration to this most bizarre of theories.

Top: The Dakota apartment building in New York City, corner of 72nd and Central Park West in Upper West Side, Manhattan. John Lennon lived here and was shot at the entrance to the building.

Above: Mark David Chapman's mugshot following his arrest. His list of alternate targets also included Paul McCartney and Ronald Reagan.

Left: A British stamp reproducing the Beatles Abbey Road album cover, an image that has intrigued some conspiracy theorists.

EVIDENCE?

CHAPMAN'S CONFUSED EXPLANATIONS FOR SHOOTING LENNON INVOLVED JD SALINGER'S NOVEL *THE CATCHER IN THE RYE* AND A BELIEF THAT LENNON CLAIMED TO BE MORE IMPORTANT THAN JESUS. CHAPMAN APPARENTLY CONTEMPLATED KILLING ELIZABETH TAYLOR OR JACKIE KENNEDY ONASSIS, BUT LENNON WAS EASIER TO FIND. CHAPMAN KILLED HIM WITH FIVE BULLETS.

IS PAUL MCCARTNEY DEAD?

Of all the rumors and conspiracy theories to surface around musicians, and the Fab Four in particular, the story that Paul McCartney died in November 1966 and was replaced with a look-alike is one of the most persistent.

Clues that Paul McCartney died have allegedly been found in Beatles songs and album artwork, with rumors circulating in 1967 and gaining in popularity in 1969 after the news spread around college campuses in America.

The rumor first started in London in early 1967, reporting that Paul McCartney had died in a traffic accident on the M1 motorway. As the story goes, the remaining Beatles decided to use a look-alike contest winner as a replacement for Paul to save their fans from heartbreak and grief. However, the band supposedly felt guilty about this and started leaving clues in their music and artwork. The assassination of John F. Kennedy in 1963 and its aftermath created a climate for conspiracy theories and, with their popularity and productivity, clues were quickly found, circulated and discussed.

In 1993, Paul McCartney parodied the theory with the title of his live album Paul Is Live, with the cover artwork itself containing several deliberate references to the conspiracy theory. Time magazine also included the "Paul is dead" conspiracy in its 2009 list of "the world's most enduring conspiracy theories."

Above: McCartney and Lennon performing in Munich, 1966.

Left: The record cover for Help raised questions when the semaphore on the front didn't actually spell out "help."

Above: Strawberry Field was a former Salvation Army children's home in Liverpool, immortalized by the Beatles.

Above: The famous album cover for *Abbey Road* was shot on this crossing. People have read meaning into the simple photograph, seeing Paul's death in a secret message.

SOME OF THE CLUES:

- *Sgt. Pepper's Lonely Hearts Club Band* features Paul playing an alter ego named "Billy Shears." Some have suggested that this wasn't an alter ego at all, but the real name of Paul's replacement.

- In the final section of the song "Strawberry Fields Forever," John Lennon says something. It's suggested that he says, "I buried Paul," although Lennon maintained that he said "cranberry sauce."

- In the song "Taxman," George Harrison gives "advice for those who die."

- John's "A Day in the Life" includes lyrics "He blew his mind out in a car," possibly alluding to Paul's death. When the song is played backwards, a recorded phrase "Paul is dead, miss him, miss him," can supposedly be heard.

- The album cover for *Abbey Road* is said to depict a funeral procession. John in white symbolizes a preacher or heavenly figure, Ringo in black is the undertaker, George in denim is the gravedigger, and Paul barefoot and out of step symbolizes the dead man.

- Also on *Abbey Road,* the VW Beetle number plate appears to be LMW 28IF. "LMW" could be "Linda McCartney Weeps" or "Linda McCartney Widow," while Paul would have been "28 if" he had still been alive.

- Another hint reportedly on the *Abbey Road* album cover is that the original artwork showed Paul, who was left-handed, holding a cigarette in his right hand, indicating he might be an impostor. The cigarette has been removed from modern reprints and re-releases of the album.

- If "Revolution 9" from *the White Album* is played backwards, it supposedly includes the message "turn me on, dead man."

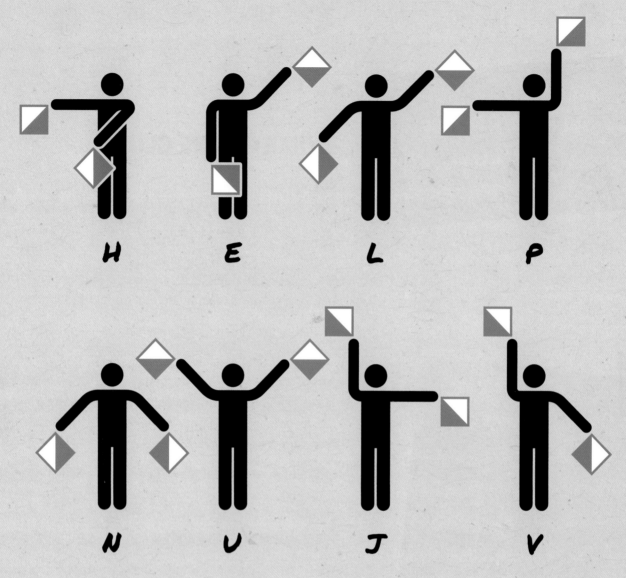

Above and left: A comparison of the semaphore for "help" and the semaphore from the front of the Beatles' album. Is this a secret message?

THE ONLY CONSPIRACY?

The artwork for the earlier 1965 album *Help!* shows the Beatles posing in semaphore. However, the word "help" wasn't liked visually, and their replacement poses instead spell out "NUJV." This gave rise to an earlier conspiracy theory that the letters stood for "New Unknown John Vocalist," leading some to believe that John had died or left the band, which had then been covered up, and that his replacement would soon take his place.

On the artwork of *With the Beatles*, Ringo's face is not on the same level as the other Beatles. Some fans interpreted this as a secret message that Ringo had in fact died.

George is the only Beatle with his back to the camera on the cover of *A Hard Day's Night*, and is also the only one smoking a cigarette. Some believed that these were signals that George had died.

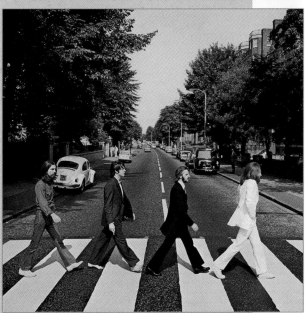

Left top, center and bottom:
The album covers for the Beatles became key points of reference for conspiracy theories. While they are all iconic, superfans believed that the band were trying to tell the fans something through their images.

IDENTITY CRISIS

Identity is key in stories of murder and mystery—not just "who did it," but "who were they?" Slipping across the pages of history are mystery men and women, around whom conspiracy theories spin webs of intrigue.

The world knows Shakespeare, or thinks it does, but did a glove-maker's son from Stratford really write all those great plays? Some argue that he didn't. So who was the man behind the famous words? Like Shakespeare, there are many we think we know about. Did you know, for example, that Dracula was inspired by a real man? We know about the witch trials, but who were the victims? Who, too, was the man in the iron mask? Jack the Ripper is another mystery figure. Millions of words have been written about him, but his identity remains unknown still today.

THE MAN IN THE IRON MASK

A famous story by Alexandre Dumas about a masked man held captive for years was based on a real historical mystery.

In 1669, Eustache Dauger was arrested in Dunkirk by soldiers of King Louis XIV of France. He spent the remaining 34 years of his life in prison, his face hidden beneath a mask, his true identity known to only a few. The solitary prisoner was guarded day and night by two musketeers, but was otherwise given comfortable treatment and was fed well.

So who was the man in the mask? (In reality, he wore a velvet hood, not the iron mask of the Dumas novel). People suspect he was in fact the king's natural father. Louis XIII's marriage to Anne of Austria was childless and for years the royal couple had lived apart, so it came as a surprise when, in 1638, the queen produced a son. The boy became king in 1643 when Louis XIII died. Rumors spread that the boy's father was not the queen's husband, but a nobleman chosen by Cardinal Richelieu, effective ruler of France, to provide France with the royal heir it needed.

Having done his duty, the bastard father may have been sent abroad, perhaps to North America, far away from the Palace of Versailles and gossip. But should he return. . . ? It seems possible that he did, as "Eustache Dauger," and if he bore a close resemblance to King Louis XIV, tongues would certainly wag. Worse, he might make his paternity known and become an embarrassment to the very regal "Sun King", busy making war across Europe.

Murder was an option, but perhaps King Louis shrank from patricide. Instead, Dauger was confined for the rest of his days, in near-silence and obscurity. When he died in 1703 in the Bastille prison in Paris, he was listed as "Eustache Dauger, valet."

EVIDENCE?

A French noblewoman described the man in the mask in a letter to England. She said he had lived and died in his mask, with no-one knowing who he was. The philosopher Voltaire suggested he was the king's illegitimate older brother. Dumas (creator of *The Three Musketeers*) dreamed up a new plot-line, that the masked man was the king's identical twin. Another theory is that he was he an Italian named Girolamo Mattioli, victim of a diplomatic mistake that upset King Louis.

Right: Pignerol, in southern France, where the Man in the Iron Mask was first held prisoner. The governor of Pignerol prison went with the prisoner whenever he moved jails, riding inside a shuttered carriage.

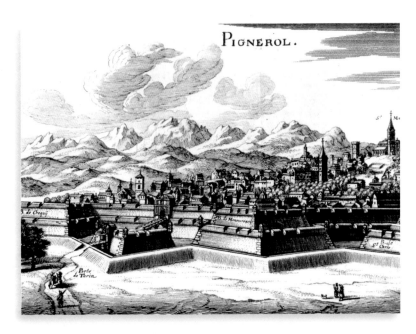

Above: King Louis XIV (1638–1715). He became King of France aged only 4, reigned for 72 years and was known as "the Sun King."

Right: A scene from the 1977 television series *The Man in the Iron Mask*, based on Dumas's classic story. In his version, there are twin brothers: one (the hero) imprisoned behind the mask, the other his brother, King Louis XIV of France. The masked man, Philippe, is the rightful heir to the throne, kept prisoner for wicked political motives, but destined to replace his brother as king.

THE REAL BLUEBEARD

Baron Gilles de Rais was a hero of medieval France until his sudden fall, when he was branded a child-killer. But was he set up?

Born in 1404, he fought alongside Joan of Arc to defeat the English; at 16 he'd married a rich heiress; at 24 he was a Marshal of France, patron of the arts and Church, second only to the King. The world was his oyster. Or so it seemed.

Having dissipated his wealth, the Baron turned to alchemy and magic to make gold from cheap metals. His enemies said he'd sold his soul to the Devil. In 1440, Gilles de Rais was accused or sorcery and child-murder, of conspiring to abduct 140 children, draining their blood in satanic rituals to make magic potions. Even in a land used to violent death and torture, such "devilry" caused shock and abhorrence.

Gilles de Rais was tried in secret. Rather than defend himself, he confessed, admitting his wicked blood-lusts and was hanged at Nantes. With so little evidence, his friends could not believe his guilt.

Above: Arthur Rackham's illustration from his *Fairy Book* (1913); Bluebeard warns his wife not to open his locked room. What horrors await inside?

Right: A portrait of Gilles de Rais, who was a war hero and fought alongside Joan of Arc. Was this all a cover for his horrific hobbies?

Below: The family seal of Gilles de Rais.

The witnesses who confessed murders and blood-rituals were probably tortured and so may Gilles de Rais have been himself. How could he have fallen so far and fast? Was he trapped by conspiring enemies, chief among them the Duke of Brittany? Gilles de Rais made an easy target with his sexual licence and interest in astrology and alchemy; all combined to create an image of a devil-worshipper. Certainly he was no saint, but a child-killer?

The family of Gilles de Rais survived the scandal of his downfall, for by admitting guilt and offering repentance, the Baron salvaged at least some of his fortune, though his castles were taken by Duke John of Brittany. By law, a portion of a repentant sinner's estate remained with his family; had Gilles de Rais fought his case and lost, they would have lost too.

EVIDENCE?

JOAN OF ARC, THE PEASANT GIRL-SOLDIER FROM DOMRÉMY, LED FRENCH SOLDIERS AGAINST THE ENGLISH WHO, AFTER AGINCOURT (1415) THREATENED TO TAKE CONTROL OF FRANCE. AT HER SIDE AT THE BATTLE OF ORLÉANS (1429) WAS THE YOUNG GILLES DE RAIS. HOWEVER, THE YOUNG WARLORD'S BRAVERY, WEALTH AND GENEROSITY POSSIBLY HID A DARKER SIDE. AFTER NEARLY 700 YEARS, IT'S HARD TO JUDGE INNOCENCE OR GUILT.

Right: Statue of St Joan of Arc, France's warrior-heroine, at Blois. The peasant girl-soldier trusted the aristocratic Gilles de Rais, who was her gallant lieutenant in battles against the English.

Above: Vlad Ţepeş has become a folk hero in Romania, where he lived. While he was known for obscene violence and cruelty, some saw him as a freedom fighter.

DRACULA

Count Dracula is known throughout the world as the fictional vampire who haunts the night, but the real Dracula was known as Vlad the Impaler, renowned through Europe because of his cruelty.

Born in Transylvania, part of modern-day Romania, Vlad III Dracula was the ruler of Walachia between 1448 and 1476. Walachia was a small principality bordered on three sides by the Danube River, and to the north by the Transylvanian Alps. His power wasn't absolute, however, and he spent most of his life battling with other nobles for the throne. In 1448, he only ruled for two months before being deposed, but after eight years of fighting he claimed the crown again. This was when he began the campaign of terror which earned him the name Vlad Ţepeş: Vlad the Impaler.

Stories of his cruelty circulated Europe even during his lifetime, leading to poems and stories being written about him. In 1462, he left a field filled with thousands of impaled victims to deter anyone pursuing his retreating army. According to other stories, he invented new tortures: boiling people to death, desecrating churches, and brutalizing families and civilians. When Dracula was captured enemy forces, rumors spread that during his time in prison he caught rats to cut up into pieces, or stick to pieces of wood just to torture them. Accounts of his acts were shared across the continent. He was described as a man of unheard cruelty, and a gruesome murderer. By today's standards, he would be guilty of war crimes, including genocide.

These rumors were collected into books and became popular in many countries, as people were horrified but also curious about this terrible man. In his homeland he remained a folk hero to many, seen as bringing order and safety to Walachia, but his violence seemed inhuman to the rest of the world. Although there was a rich culture of vampire legend in Walachia, however, there is nothing to suggest that Dracula was anything other than a human—except, perhaps, in his exceptional cruelty.

Left: Bram Stoker claimed not to know much of Vlad Ţepeş when he wrote *Dracula*, instead choosing a name almost at random. But can that be true when Dracula had such a history of violence?

VLAD ȚEPEȘ
1431-1476
DOMNITOR AL ȚĂRII ROMÂNEȘTI
ÎNTRE ANII
1448 : 1456 — 1462 : 1476

Above: Plaques in Romania mark where Țepeș lived, and it is a popular tourist destination.

Above: Bela Lugosi was famous for portraying the vampire count throughout his career, and is partly responsible for his iconic appearance.

WAS SHAKESPEARE A PEN NAME?

William Shakespeare's plays are the greatest ever staged. True, but who wrote them—the actor from Stratford or someone else?

Little is known of Shakespeare's life other than the bare facts: a glovemaker's son born in Stratford upon Avon in 1564, he married and had three children, went to London after 1585 and by 1592 was an actor, prolific dramatist (at least 37 plays) and co-founder of the Globe Theatre. Rich and successful, he retired to Stratford, where he died in 1616.

"Anti-Stratfordians" claimed that no mere actor, with a grammar school education, could have written plays of such wit, erudition and insight. Francis Bacon was put forward as Shakespeare as early as 1785, followed in the 1920s by Edward de Vere, Earl of Oxford and in the 1950s by William Stanley Earl of Derby. Christopher Marlowe, a playwright who died just as Shakespeare was getting well-known, is another candidate. Bacon, Oxford and Derby are argued to have used pen-names to avoid the social stigma associated with public theatre. The arguments against Shakespeare are largely based on the view that he must have lacked the education and breadth of experience, especially of classical literature, history and travel, that a nobleman might have and which is evident in the plays.

In 1796, London's star actor John Kemble presented "a new play by Shakespeare" at the Drury Lane Theatre. Titled *Vortigern and Rowena*, the play had in fact just been written by a 17-year-old faker named William Henry Ireland. Kemble suspected Vortigern was a fraud and mid-performance the tittering audience caught on that the leading actor was hamming up "this solemn mockery." The play closed on its opening night. Undeterred, Ireland continued to pen Shakespeare plays as well as writing under his own name.

Above: Actors in Moscow perform *Hamlet* in a Russian Army production. Shakespeare's appeal is international and his authorship seldom questioned outside academic circles.

EVIDENCE?

Statesman and scientist Francis Bacon was a brilliant writer; his supporters claim there are "Baconisms" in Shakespeare which could only have been provided by him. Oxford and Stanley were poets and Derby patron of an actors' company. Marlowe wrote plays of early genius before being murdered in 1793 in a tavern brawl. But was it really Marlowe who died or a substitute "fall-guy"? If Marlowe was a government agent, perhaps, some suggest, he was spirited away to exile in Italy to carry on writing as Shakespeare.

Above: The modern Globe theatre in London, a reconstruction of the playhouse in which many of Shakespeare's plays were first performed and in which he was a partner.

Right: William Shakespeare, the boy from a country town in the heart of England who went to London—and made good. Genius can defy explanation.

Below: Jack the Ripper struck at night, murdering prostitutes and mutilating their bodies.

WHO WAS JACK THE RIPPER?

The Whitechapel murders of 1888 spread fear through London's East End. The identity of Jack the Ripper remains unknown.

Five murders in 1888 were almost certainly the Ripper's and two or three others are possible. All the victims were female, all were prostitutes, almost all the bodies were mutilated and some had body organs removed. All the killings were done in the same area and over a few months. Was there a conspiracy to cover up the killer's identity? Were there more murders and why did it take many years for some bits of evidence to reach the public domain?

The Metropolitan Police received taunting letters signed "Jack the Ripper." The first letter, dated September 25, 1888, boasted "my knife is nice and sharp," and one sent on October 16 contained a human kidney. The police were inundated with names of suspects. But were any of them the Ripper?

The police had little to go on other than blood-soaked scenes of crime. Scanty witness evidence suggested the killer was a white male. Could he be a surgeon? A madman? A seaman? A crazed abortionist? Even Prince Albert Victor, Duke of Clarence and the royal physician Sir William Gull were proposed. Adherents of the royal-killer theory suggested the prince was being blackmailed by one of the victims and that the government, in league with the Freemasons, moved to silence her and her friends. Was Antisemitism involved? A chalked message mentioning "Juwes" was hurriedly erased by police. Sir Melville Macnaghten (who did not join Scotland Yard until after the murders) privately listed his suspects. They included Montague Druitt, a teacher who had lost his job and drowned himself in 1888.

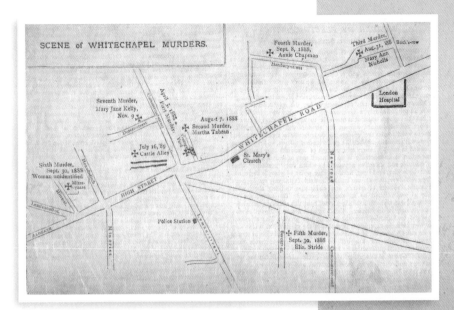

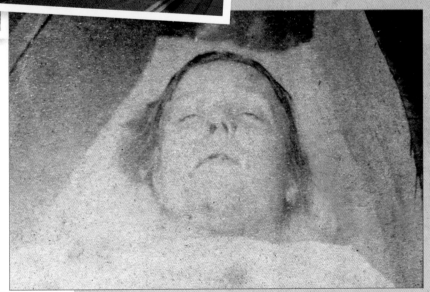

Above: The Ripper murders were committed within a relatively small area of London's East End. The Whitechapel Road ran through the heart of the crime scene.

Above: Bucks Row (now Durward Street) as it was when the body of Mary Ann Nichols was found in 1888 and as it is today. The tall school building can be seen in both pictures.

Right: A police photograph of Ripper victim Mary Ann Nichols, killed on August 31, 1888.

Above: James Maybrick, a Liverpool cotton merchant, was killed by his wife in 1889. His diary, revealed in 1994, purports to record the Ripper killings, but is not taken very seriously.

Above: Prince Albert Victor, Duke of Clarence (1864–92) was a grandson of Queen Victoria. Evidence suggests he was not in London at the time of the Ripper murders.

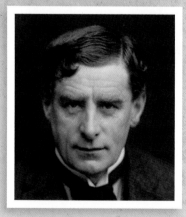

Above: Walter Sickert (1860–1942), seen here in a 1911 photo, was suggested as the Ripper by crime writer Patricia Cornwell.

Apart from Druitt, other suspects included artist Walter Sickert, who painted a picture of "Jack the Ripper's Bedroom"; Aaron Kosminski, certified insane in 1891; Nathan Kaminski, who died in an asylum in 1889; and James Maybrick, poisoned by his wife in 1889. Also suggested are Michael Ostrog, Russian con-man; John Pizer or "Leather Apron," a thug who extorted money from prostitutes; and William Bury, hanged in 1889 for murdering his wife. Detective Frederick Abberline suspected George Chapman (aka Severin Klosowski), a Polish hairdresser, hanged in 1903 for murder.

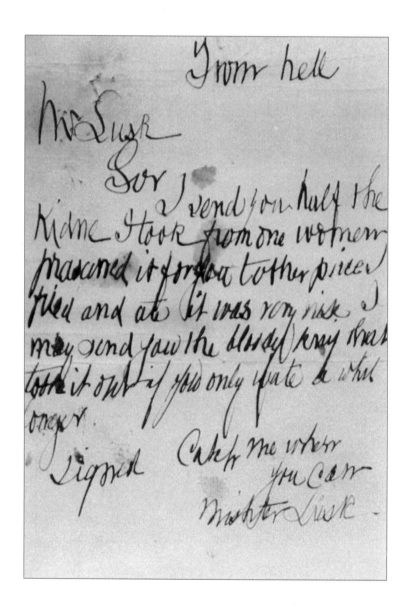

Above: The "From Hell" letter, in which the writer mentions a kidney he has removed from one of his victim and eaten. Although there were numerous hoax letters, the police thought this one was probably genuine.

Below: This is a page from the Macnaghten memorandum of 1894, in response to a newspaper allegation that a man named Thomas Cutbush was the Ripper. Macnaghten listed his main suspects: Druitt, Kosminski and Ostrog.

Above: The Ripper murders featured in this edition of The Illustrated Police News, published in London on December 8, 1888.

Above: Fashionable men read about the Ripper murders and wondered, was any one of their class responsible for butchering the Whitechapel prostitutes?

SALEM WITCH TRIALS

In Salem, Massachusetts, between February 1692 and May 1693, more than two hundred people were accused of witchcraft. But was the village riddled with witches, was it just neighbors bickering, or was it something more co-coordinated?

The witch trials have become famous for mass hysteria and paranoia in American history. Of the 200 people accused, 30 were found guilty, and 19 were hanged for their crimes: 14 women and five men. A further man was pressed to death (crushed under a board piled with heavy rocks) because he refused to plead, and at least five others died in jail.

Many people believe that these trials and accusations were an attempt by the Puritan church to control women and religious dissidents, and to gain political control. Books written by Increase Mather and his son Cotton Mather were published in 1684 and 1689, detailing the evils of witchcraft and demons. Increase Mather was involved in government in the UK and claimed to have appointed all the new government members for the Province of Massachusetts Bay. This included the new Governor, William Phips, who had worked with Mather in London. Phips didn't arrive in Massachusetts until May 1692, several months after the witch trials began, but word had been sent in January. Were the trials an attempt by local officials to gain political favor with the new Governor?

Above: The home of Judge Jonathan Corwin, who presided over the trials in Salem, is commemorated with a sign marking it as a Witch House.

Below: Contemporary stories fueled the fires of witch hunts, telling tales of witches who used their magic during the trials to try and enact their revenge on those judging them.

Left: Martha Cory was jailed for witchcraft in 1692. As a witch, she was given no access to a lawyer to defend herself, and though she maintained her innocence she was found guilty and hanged.

The colonies in America in the 1600s were formed initially by members of the Puritan church, leaving England to form a new religious state more in line with their views. This religious sincerity meant that anything seen as sinful could be punished harshly, and quarrels between neighbors could be escalated to potentially deadly ends. That, combined with rising hysteria about the presence of witches, could have created a feedback loop of fear and accusation. The more witches accused, the more people feared witches, and the more people thought they saw them. Was this fear fanned by officials to exert power? Or did conniving townspeople take advantage of the situation to remove people they disliked?

Modern historians have suggested that some of the panic around the witch trials could have been caused by illnesses which developed as a result of eating infected grain. Claviceps purpurea has been found in rye bread commonly eaten at the time, and is the fungus which LSD is derived from. Were hallucinations as a result of a natural psychotropic drug the cause? If that was true, why did people confess to witchcraft?

In reality, all of these factors probably played a part. In 1711, a number of victims were exonerated by the government and their families offered recompense, although none claimed it. Another victim, Ann Pudeator, was cleared by the state of Massachusetts in 1957, and five of the women executed for witchcraft were fully exonerated by the state in 2001.

CONFESSION OF SALEM JURORS, &c.

From Calef's "Salem Witchcraft." Page 294.

" Some that had been of several Juries, have given forth a paper, signed with their own hands, in these words :

" WE whose names are under written, being in the year 1692, called to serve as jurors in court at *Salem* on trial of many ; who were by some suspected guilty of doing acts of witchcraft upon the bodies of sundry persons.

" We confess that we ourselves were not capable to understand, nor able to withstand the mysterious delusions of the powers of darkness, and prince of the air ; but were, for want of knowledge in ourselves, and better information from others, prevailed with to take up with such evidence against the accused, as on further consideration, and better information, we justly fear, was insufficient for the touching the lives of any : Deut. xvii. 6., whereby we fear we have been instrumental with others, though ignorantly and unwittingly, to bring upon ourselves and this people of the Lord, the guilt of innocent blood ; which sin the Lord saith in scripture, he would not pardon : 2 Kings xxiv. 4 ; that is, we suppose in regard of his temporal judgment. We do therefore hereby signify to all in general (and to the surviving sufferers in special) our deep sense of, and sorrow for our errors, in acting on such evidence to the condemning of any person.

" And do hereby declare that we justly fear that we were sadly deluded and mistaken, for which we are much disquieted and distressed in our minds ; and do therefore humbly beg forgiveness, first of God for Christ's sake for this our error ; and pray that God would not impute the guilt of it to ourselves nor others ; and we also pray that we may be considered candidly, and aright by the living sufferers as being then under the power of a strong and general delusion, utterly unacquainted with, and not experienced in matters of that nature.

" We do heartily ask forgiveness of you all, whom we have justly offended, and do declare according to our present minds, we would none of us do such things again on such grounds for the whole world ; praying you to accept of this in way of satisfaction for our offence ; and that you would bless the inheritance of the Lord, that he may be entreated for the land.

" Foreman, THOMAS FISK,   THOMAS PERLY, Sen.,
  WILLIAM FISK,   JOHN PEBODY,
  JOHN BACHELER,   THOMAS PERKINS,
  THOMAS FISK, Jun.,   SAMUEL SAYER,
  JOHN DANE,   ANDREW ELLIOTT,
  JOSEPH EVELITH,   HENRY HERRICK, Sen."
[Not dated.]

Above: This page from *Strange Phenomena of New England In the Seventeenth Century, Including the Salem Witchcraft,* 1692, details confessions from jurors who admitted that the women prosecuted were not tried fairly.

BRITISH WITCHES

The Salem witch trials were not the first of their kind. Throughout the 1500s, witch trials were taking place across Europe. In Britain, King James I was known for his dislike of witches. He wrote a book called *Daemonologie*, discussing the evils of witchcraft and devil worship. In 1563, the Scottish Parliament had passed the Witchcraft Act, which made both practicing witchcraft and consulting witches capital crimes. The first witch hunt under this law was between 1568 and 1569. Over the years Scotland tried somewhere between 4000 and 6000 people for witchcraft, a far higher rate than Salem. Nearly three quarters of the accused were women, and it is estimated that 1500 were executed. Some confessed, but only after torture.

When Elizabeth I died and James VI of Scotland also became James I of England, the witch trials moved south. It was believed that in many places local lawmakers pursued witch trials to gain favour with the new king. The most famous of these are the Pendle Witch Trials, which took place in Lancashire in 1612. Twelve people were accused of witchcraft. One died in prison, and of the eleven who stood trial only one was found innocent. The remaining ten were executed by hanging.

For the Pendle witches in particular, historians believe that it was sparked by a quarrel between two families—the Devices and the Chattoxes. Demdike Device and Anne Chattox were rivals as local "wise women," who acted as witches, and made money through begging and making spells for their neighbors. Many of the accusations against them came from members of their own families. In fact, a key witness against the Devices was their youngest daughter, Jennet Device. 22 years later, Jennet herself was accused of witchcraft and the murder of Isabelle Nutter, a relative of Anne Chattox. She was imprisoned, but not executed.

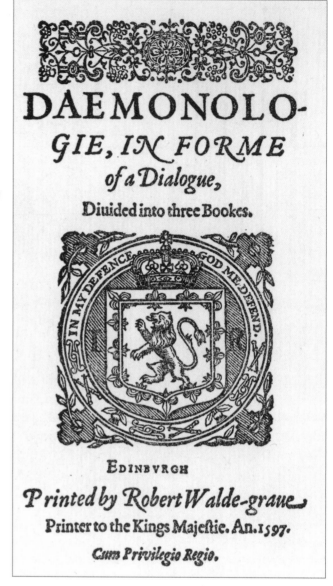

Above: James VI of Scotland (James I of England) wrote a book on devil worship and witchcraft which was used as reference in many British witch trials.

Right: In Lancashire, UK you can walk a memorial path to the Pendle witches.

Other trials took place throughout England into the 1700s, but nothing on the scale of the Scottish witch hunts. In 2004, 81 witches from the Scottish trials were pardoned. What of the others who were killed? Unlike Salem, the British witch trials have presented no evidence of hallucinogenic substances to promote hysteria, so it seems likely that these trials were entirely for personal and political gain.

Above: A memorial in Scotland to one of the women executed during the witch hunts.

Left: An illustration from *Daemonology* showing witches being brought for judgment.

MYTHICAL CREATURES

For centuries, rumors of strange creatures have captured our imaginations. Evidence is often scarce or unreliable, yet our fondness and even belief about such things continue as questions continue to be asked and mysteries continue.

Despite our shrinking world and expanding scientific knowledge, there still seems to be room for belief in unknown creatures—such as the Yeti, Bigfoot, and the Loch Ness Monster—that keep academic establishments guessing. The story of "the one that got away" is often the most entertaining. Some stories and even evidence are dismissed as a hoax, although conspiracy theorists will argue that what science dismisses as a hoax is sometimes the truth.

THE FEEJEE MERMAID

The mermaid of myth is beautiful and often wistful, but the mermaids exhibited at fairs and freak shows were a very different kettle of fish.

Mermaids in folklore are half-woman, half-fish, though in some tales they can live on land and even become human. Mermaids and mermen were rather like fairies: magical but not immortal, without souls but drawn to people, sometimes fatally. Mermaids' songs could lure sailors to their dooms, though a man might marry a mermaid and keep her if he stole her comb and mirror or her cap and belt. So long as he kept them hidden, his mermaid-lover would remain with him.

A celebrated medieval mermaid was said to have been found in 1403 on mudflats at Edam in Holland. Befriended by village women, she lived 15 years and was given a Christian burial in the churchyard, but never learned to speak. Cornwall is particularly rich in mermaid stories, such as the Mermaid of Zennor, who fell in love with a local man.

Not surprisingly, hoaxers and charlatans cashed in with fake mermaids that in most cases looked so hideous that few people could have been convinced by them. Taxidermists and showmen combined to wow the public with grotesque creations put together from bits of fish, lizard, pig and monkey. In the 19th century, Japanese fishermen did a flourishing trade selling dead fish-monkey mermaids. Perhaps the most celebrated mermaid was displayed by American impresario and circus man P. T. Barnum in 1842. Advertised as the "Feejee Mermaid," and purportedly caught by a Dr Griffin, the exhibit toured country shows and fairs across the United States. It was later acquired by Harvard University's Peabody Museum of Archaeology and Ethnology. The mummified mermaid turned out to be just another shriveled fake.

Above: Phineas T. Barnum (1810–1891), whose attractions included General Tom Thumb and Jumbo the elephant. He once claimed to have exhibited George Washington's nurse.

THE TRUTH?

SAILORS CAME HOME WITH STORIES OF STRANGE SEA MONSTERS, NONE MORE TERRIFYING THAN THE KRAKEN, AS BIG AS AN ISLAND, WITH TENTACLES THAT DRAGGED DOWN SHIPS. THE GIANT SQUID CAN GROW TO VAST SIZE BUT LIVES IN THE OCEAN DEEPS AND, DESPITE ITS STARRING ROLE IN FILMS SUCH AS 20,000 LEAGUES UNDER THE SEA, IS UNLIKELY TO WRESTLE WITH A SHIP!

Above: A statue of Syrene, a war-like mermaid in Warsaw's Market Square originally created in 1850 to echo the mermaid on the city's coat of arms.

Left: The Banff Merman is kept in a glass case at the Canadian city's Indian Trading Post. A shipping bill suggests the store's former owner bought a "man-fish" from Java, but it may well have been a home-made hoax.

Above: The un-alluring Feejee Mermaid, a grisly composite of paper, glue, stuffing, fish-tail, baby orangutan and monkey-head, dried and crinkled.

THE LOCH NESS MONSTER

Loch Ness in Scotland is more than 300 m (900 ft) deep. In 1934, a London doctor on holiday took a photograph of a snaky neck and head protruding from the peaty waters. The picture of a "monster" caused a sensation.

More sightings followed, such as when local resident Lachlan Stuart, up early for morning milking in 1951, spotted three humps. In 1960, Tim Dinsdale shot the first moving pictures of "Nessie," and in 1961 the Loch Ness Phenomena Investigation Bureau set up observers and cameras around the loch to try and establish if there really were creatures lurking in its murky depths.

Nessie remained unseen until, in 1975, Robert Rines produced film that convinced naturalist Peter Scott that there was a genuine unknown species: it appeared reddish-brown, about 4 m (13 ft) long and had an arching neck and flippers. Could a small population of prehistoric plesiosaurs have survived in Loch Ness? After all, there were tales of other Scottish lake beasts, such as the Mhorag of Loch Morar.

The Rines images sparked worldwide interest, though geologists ridiculed any pre-Ice Age survivor theory. Sonar scans picked up occasional unidentified tracks or objects, but, in 2003, a survey for the BBC using sonar and satellite technology found nothing. Images continued to surface. In 2007, Gordon Holmes videoed "something about 13 m (45 ft) long," though this sighting was challenged, as was a 2011 photo of something trailing a boat, dismissed by skeptics as a mass of weed. In 2008, Dr Rines concluded that Nessie might be extinct. Without a body, the Loch Ness Monster remains, in Scottish legal terms, "not proven."

Above: A postcard of Loch Ness bearing the words "The haunts of the Monster" invites tourists to peer closer.

Below: Many visitors are drawn to Loch Ness hoping to catch a glimpse of something strange swimming in the loch.

Left: Taken in 1934 by Colonel R. K. Wilson, a London surgeon, this famous photograph was said to show the Loch Ness Monster swimming. Only in the 1990s was the photo revealed to be a hoax—Wilson and friends had rigged a toy submarine with a model head.

EVIDENCE?

Dr George Zug, reptile expert at the Smithsonian Institution in the United States, gave his opinion of the Rines images: "I believe these data indicate the presence of large animals in Loch Ness, but are insufficient to identify them." It seems unlikely that any large animals, prehistoric or modern, could thrive in Loch Ness, unless swimming in and out through subterranean rivers to the sea. Prosaic explanations for the Loch Ness monster include decaying plant matter, waves and water eddies and mistaken sightings of seals or otters.

Main: If the Loch Ness monster was actually a plesiosaur that had somehow outlived the dinosaurs, it may look something like this as it swims in the depths of the very deep Scottish loch.

Above: Sketches of Piltdown Man, based on reconstructions published in 1913, when scientists were persuaded that Charles Dawson had unearthed a genuine "missing link" in human evolution.

PILTDOWN MAN

Piltdown Man is one of the most famous hoaxes in palaeontology. For some 40 years, it fooled the scientific establishment, who thought that a "missing link" in human evolution been discovered.

Piltdown Man wasn't in fact a whole man, merely fragments of a skull and jawbone. In December 1912, newspaper headlines revealing the 1908 discovery in a gravel pit in southern England caused a sensation.

For centuries, the fossil evidence for prehistoric life had puzzled people. Fossils dug up by farmers were explained away as the remains of dragons, giants or animals drowned in Noah's Flood. In the early 1800s, finds of extinct giant reptiles led to an outbreak of "dinosaur fever," but exactly how humans had evolved remained a mystery.

Then, in 1912, what appeared to be a prehistoric "skull" was discovered in Sussex. The Manchester Guardian newspaper called the find "by far the earliest trace of mankind that has yet been found in England." Piltdown man, named after a village in Sussex, seemed to be the "missing link" between apes and humans.

The find was credited to local solicitor and fossil-hunter Charles Dawson and named eoanthropus dawsoni. Dawson claimed more finds: a tooth in 1913 and another tooth and more bones in 1915. He died in 1916, but Piltdown Man's place in history seemed secure. In 1950, a reconstruction of a head was made based on the bones. Then, in 1953, just as Britain was celebrating the conquest of Everest and the coronation of Elizabeth II, "Piltdown Man" was declared a fake. People questioned how such a hoax could have escaped detection without the compliance of an expert.

THE TRUTH?

A NUMBER OF PEOPLE CAME UNDER SUSPICION AS BEING THE CREATOR OF THE FAKE FOSSIL. ONE SUSPECT WAS DAWSON, WHO WAS KNOWN TO HAVE FAKED FOSSILS. ANOTHER WAS MARTIN HINTON, WHO WORKED AT THE NATURAL HISTORY MUSEUM. HINTON HAD MADE TESTS ON BONE-STAINS, BUT WAS HE A HOAXER OR A DETECTIVE? HINTON AND DAWSON MAY HAVE CONSPIRED TO FOOL SIR ARTHUR SMITH WOODWARD OF THE MUSEUM. WRITER AND FOSSIL-HUNTER SIR ARTHUR CONAN DOYLE WAS ANOTHER SUSPECT. IT WAS THOUGHT HE MAY HAVE BEEN KEEN TO GET HIS OWN BACK ON SCIENTISTS WHO HAD RIDICULED HIS HIGH-PROFILE INTEREST IN GHOSTS, SPIRITS AND THE AFTERLIFE.

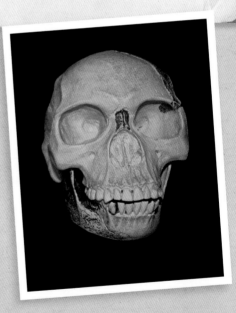

Left: Discoverers and diggers pose at the discovery site near Piltdown in Sussex, southern England.

Above: Reconstruction of the Piltdown skull. Tests in 1949 showed that the skull was not prehistoric after all. It had been faked from an orangutan's lower jawbone and human bones of medieval origin, boiled and stained to look more ancient.

Above: Hapless hoax or hairy hominid, Bigfoot has set his feet firmly into some tracts of North American culture—even to the extent of inspiring warning signs on highways!

Below: The fossil jaw of the extinct primate Gigantopithecus blacki. Some Bigfoot proponents have suggested that sightings of Bigfoot could be relict populations of this giant prehistoric ape-man.

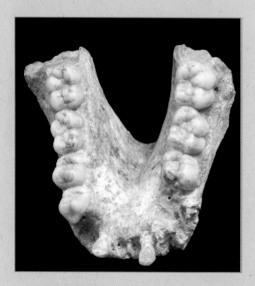

BIGFOOT

Do large, hairy creatures really lurk in the woods of North America? Numerous hunts for Bigfoot have failed to find the hairy wild men.

Bigfoot is supposed to haunt the forests of the American and Canadian Northwest. Said to be 2–3 m (6–10 ft) tall, heavier than a man, with huge feet, shaggy hair and a repulsive smell, its other name is Sasquatch, from a First Nation/Native American word sasq'ets. The Sasquatch first hit the press in Canada in the 1920s, after sensational stories were reported of miners and monsters in the woods. One miner claimed he'd been abducted by a Bigfoot and another that he and his companions were attacked by ape-men hurling rocks. The stories were dismissed as hoaxes or practical jokes, possibly played by student campers.

More reports of sightings and footprints were made during the 1950s, along with further hoax allegations. Bigfoot paw-prints found at Bluff Creek, California, in 1958, were made by wooden feet, according to the family of Bigfoot-hunter and hoaxer Raymond Wallace (1918–2002), who is known to have faked Bigfoot hair using the hair from a bison.

Of hundreds of Bigfoot sightings, the most famous was in 1967, filmed by Roger Patterson and Robert Gimlin at Eureka, California. Captured on 16 mm (0.6 in.) film is what looks like a hairy female humanoid, walking erect and swinging its arms before hurrying off into the woods. The film aroused great excitement and violent arguments. Did the film show a genuine "cryptid" or unknown animal or was it a hoax? Bob Heironimus, a friend of Patterson's, later said Bigfoot was really him in an ape-suit, but Patterson and Gimlin refused to own up. Bigfoot was also spotted further east, in Illinois, where in 1973 a couple in a parked car were scared out of their wits by a roaring, hairy, slime-dripping creature that entered local folklore as the Murphysboro Mud Monster. The foul smell they described seemed to show affinities with the Sasquatch!

Above: A mold of a skull believed to be Bigfoot's found in a display case in the Bigfoot Discovery Museum, California.

Right: The most famous Bigfoot sighting was staged by a man in a hairy ape-suit!

EVIDENCE?

PHOTOGRAPHS TAKEN IN 2007 OF A MYSTERIOUS HAIRY PRIMATE WERE, ACCORDING TO SCIENTISTS, MOST LIKELY TO BE A BEAR WITH MANGE, THOUGH SOME SUGGESTED THE LIMBS LOOKED MORE LIKE A CHIMPANZEE'S. IN 2014, SCIENTISTS FROM OXFORD UNIVERSITY CONDUCTED THE FIRST GENETIC TESTS ON HAIR SAMPLES CLAIMED TO BE FROM BIGFOOT. THE RESULTS REVEALED THAT THEY ALL CAME FROM BEARS AND OTHER KNOWN MAMMALS, NOT FROM AN UNKNOWN APE OR HOMINOID-LIKE CREATURE.

THE YETI

High in the world's highest mountains lives the elusive Yeti, also known as the "abominable snowman." Or does it?

Stories of "wild men of the woods" abound, but the Yeti (if it exists) has a particularly inaccessible habitat—the high Himalayas. The first known European report of a Yeti was in 1832, when a British official in Nepal described an unknown hairy creature that walked erect. In 1921, the name "abominable snowman" was coined by Western climbers, striving to conquer the world's greatest mountain peaks and enthralled by local tales of the "Yeti," also called Minka or "wild man" and Kang-Admi or "snow man."

In 1948, a Norwegian claimed he'd been attacked by two Yetis in Sikkim. In 1951, British climber Eric Shipton took photos of Yeti footprints in the snow in the Gauri Sankar range. Most experts concluded the prints were those of a bear, possibly distorted as the snow melted. Local sherpas were happy to recount stories of the Yeti, and monks in a Himalayan monastery showed off Yeti bones, skins and scalps and even a thumb. Edmund Hillary and Tenzing Norgay saw strange footprints in 1953, during the first ascent of Everest, though both remained skeptics. An expedition mounted in 1960 by Hillary failed to find proof of the Yeti's existence.

Some people speculate that tiny populations of prehistoric primates such as Gigantopithecus might have found sanctuary in the high Himalayas, far from people and suggest the North American Bigfoot as a similar "wild man" survivor. Few scientists give this theory credit, though and most believe Yetis are more likely bears, monkeys, foxes or snow leopards.

Above: An illustration from a 1954 French magazine, showing Sherpas being woken by a Yeti in their tent.

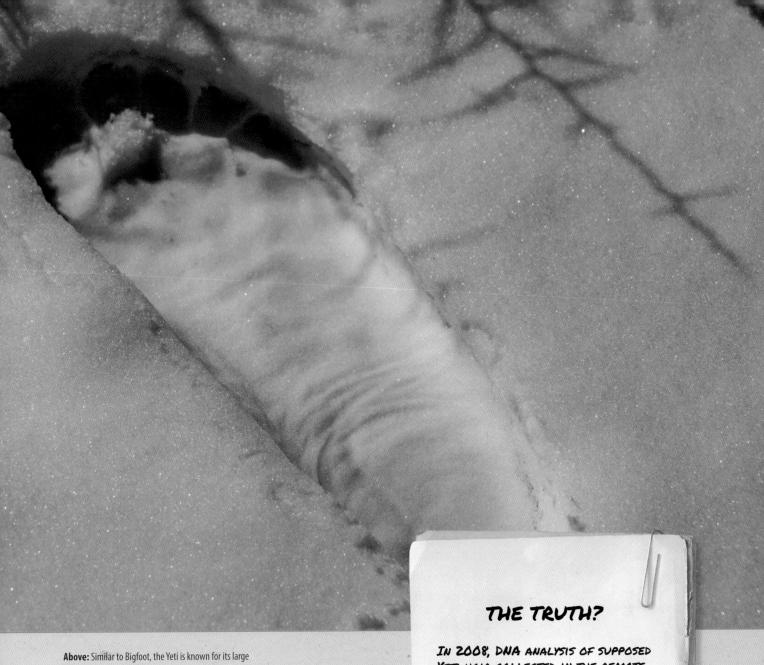

Above: Similar to Bigfoot, the Yeti is known for its large footprints, left in the snow.

Below: Himalayan monks preserve what some people claim are Yeti body parts. This scalp of a Yeti is kept under lock and key at Khumjung monastery in Nepal.

THE TRUTH?

IN 2008, DNA ANALYSIS OF SUPPOSED YETI HAIR COLLECTED IN THE REMOTE HILLS OF NORTHEAST INDIA SHOWED IT CAME NOT FROM A YETI BUT FROM THE HIMALAYAN GORAL, A GOAT-LIKE ANIMAL.

IN DECEMBER 2011, BORDER PATROL SOLDIERS IN RUSSIA ACTUALLY CAPTURED AN ALLEGED YETI, A TWO-LEGGED CREATURE 2 METERS (6FT 7IN) TALL. IT WAS LATER REVEALED AS AN ELABORATE HOAX.

FAIRIES AT THE BOTTOM OF THE GARDEN

In July 1917, two girls in a Yorkshire village took photographs of the fairies in their garden. For many years people wondered if the Cottingley Fairies were really evidence of another world or simply a children's prank.

Above: An illustration from the book of fairy tales used by Frances and Elsie.

Cousins Elsie Wright (16) and Frances Griffiths (10) were at the Wrights' home in Cottingley, near Bradford, Yorkshire, when they got wet playing by the stream. They gave the excuse that they'd been "playing with fairies," and to prove it persuaded Elsie's father to lend them his new camera.

The first photograph showed Frances with four fairies. Weeks later the girls took a photograph of Elsie with a gnome. In 1919 Mrs Wright showed the fairy pictures to the local Theosophical Society in Bradford. As a Theosophist, Mrs Wright was inclined toward a belief in a spirit-world; in the years following the mass slaughter of the First World War, many people had turned toward such beliefs. Fellow-Theosophist Edward Gardner believed he was looking at photographic evidence of "spiritual evolution" and in the summer of 1920 he asked the girls to try again. With a different camera, the girls took three new pictures, unobserved by adults: the first showed Frances with a leaping fairy; the second showed Elsie being offered flowers by a fairy; and the third was a picture of "Fairies and their Sun-Bath."

The photos caused much excitement. In 1921, the writer and spiritualist Sir Arthur Conan Doyle, of *Sherlock Holmes* fame, published the Cottingley photographs in an article on fairies in the *Strand Magazine*. He went on to write a book about them. Gardner and clairvoyant Geoffrey Hodson tried again, but no fairies came out to be photographed and the girls later admitted having fun at Hodson's expense.

Photography experts argued about the fairy photos. Could the fairies possibly be genuine? Skeptics pointed out that they looked too much like "illustrated fairies," with fashionable hairstyles. Supporters could not believe that eminent people such as Conan Doyle could be taken in by children.

Above: Frances Wright with the "leaping fairy," taken in 1920. Of the two girls, Frances was the most reluctant to own up to a hoax.

THE TRUTH?

GARDNER AND CONAN DOYLE ASKED KODAK EXPERTS TO VALIDATE THE FAIRY PHOTOS. THE VERDICT WAS THAT, ALTHOUGH THERE WERE NO OBVIOUS SIGNS OF FAKING, THE IMAGES WERE NOT NECESSARILY OF REAL FAIRIES. SINCE THERE WERE NO SUCH THINGS AS FAIRIES, A KODAK TECHNICIAN SUGGESTED, THE PHOTOS MUST BE FAKED "SOMEHOW."

Above: Cottingley Beck waterfall in Yorkshire, where the girls claimed they saw their fairies.

The girls grew up, married, lived abroad, and were almost forgotten, until, in the 1980s, they were interviewed again—and changed their story. They admitted the fairies were a joke, which they'd been amazed to find taken seriously. They had cut the fairies from a children's book, fixed them in position with hatpins, then photographed them. Elsie maintained, however, that one photo (the fifth) was indeed genuine.

Above: Frances with four fairies, in the first of the Cottingley fairy photographs.

Right: The photograph was taken on a camera like this, which was provided by Edward Gardner.

Above: The story of the Cottingley Fairies was made into a film in 1997, starring Florence Hoath.

The Evidence for Fairies
by
A. CONAN DOYLE
WITH MORE FAIRY PHOTOGRAPHS

199

This article was written by Sir A. Conan Doyle before actual photographs of fairies were known to exist. His departure for Australia prevented him from revising the article in the new light which has so strikingly strengthened his case. We are glad to be able to set before our readers two new fairy photographs, taken by the same girls, but of more recent date than those which created so much discussion when they were published in our Christmas number, and of even greater interest and importance. They speak for themselves.

WE are accustomed to the idea of amphibious creatures who may dwell unseen and unknown in the depths of the waters, and then some day be spied sunning themselves upon a sandbank, whence they slip into the unseen once more. If such appearances were rare, and if it should so happen that some saw them more clearly than others, then a very pretty controversy would arise, for the sceptics would say, with every show of reason, "Our experience is that only land creatures live on the land, and we utterly refuse to believe in things which slip in and out of the water; if you will demonstrate them to us we will begin to consider the question." Faced by so reasonable an opposition, the others could only mutter that they had seen them with their own eyes, but that they could not command their movements. The sceptics would hold the field.

Something of the sort may exist in our psychic arrangements. One can well imagine that there is a dividing line, like the water edge, this line depending upon what we vaguely call a higher rate of vibrations. Taking the vibration theory as a working hypothesis, one could conceive that by raising or lowering them, creatures could move from one side to the other of this line of material visibility, as the tortoise moves from water to the land, returning for refuge to invisibility as the reptile scuttles back to the surf. This, of course, is supposition, but intelligent supposition based on the available evidence is the pioneer of science, and it may be that the actual solution will be found in this direction. I am alluding now, not to spirit return, where seventy years of close observation has given us some sort of certain and definite laws, but rather to those fairy and phantom phenomena which have been endorsed by so many ages, and still even in these material days seem to break into some lives in the most unexpected fashion.

Victorian science would have left the world hard and clean and bare, like a landscape in the moon; but this science is in truth but a little light in the darkness, and outside that limited circle of definite knowledge we see the loom and shadow of gigantic and fantastic possibilities around us, throwing themselves continually across our consciousness in such ways that it is difficult to ignore them.

Copyright, 1921, by A. Conan Doyle.

Above and left: Sir Arthur Conan Doyle (1859-1930). The famous writer turned to spiritualism after the deaths of his son and other family members during the First World War. He wrote a lot about the existence of the supernatural, and believed the Cottingley Fairies to be real.

EVIDENCE

THE PHOTOS WERE REAL PHOTOS, BUT WERE THE FAIRIES ON THE ORIGINAL NEGATIVES OR WERE THEY ADDED LATER? BOTH THE PHOTOS AND FAIRIES WERE REAL ENOUGH; HOWEVER, THE FAIRIES WERE JUST PAPER CUTOUTS, TRACED BY THE GIRLS FROM ILLUSTRATIONS IN *PRINCESS MARY'S GIFT BOOK*

UNFINISHED JOURNEYS

Accidents by air and sea are far less common than road accidents, and complete disappearances are rarer still, but these unfinished journeys always make the news.

Usually the cause of tragedy is clear cut, but confusion and conspiracy shrouds some of the most celebrated disasters in transport history. Investigators pore over mangled wreckages, seeking to establish the truth, amid an ongoing media and internet discussion of possible causes and conspiracy suspects. Conspiracy allegations have been aired about the fate of three airlines in recent decades: TWA Flight 800 and Malaysia Airlines MH370 and MH17, whose stories are told here. Historically, disappearances in the days of sail were relatively more commonplace, sometimes blamed on sea monsters or even mermaids. When rumors congregate in specific areas, myths are born such as those about the Bermuda Triangle. Occasionally a ship would be found intact, yet without any life abroad, as in the case of the *Mary Celeste*. Today, stories such as these continue to fascinate and intrigue.

Above: The *USS Cyclops* vanished in 1918, probably overwhelmed by a storm or even a giant wave.

THE BERMUDA TRIANGLE

There is one area of the Atlantic Ocean, the so-called Bermuda Triangle, where a number of ships and planes have vanished over the years, apparently for no good reason. Does the Triangle conceal a dark secret?

The area in question is a sector of ocean between Bermuda, Florida and Puerto Rico. Here some people suggest, ships and planes are lured to disaster. Could they be the victims of unknown natural forces or darker supernatural ones?

Media interest in the Triangle was sparked in March 1918, when the *USS Cyclops* vanished—probably in a storm—with the loss of 309 crew and passengers. Interest revived in 1945, when five U.S. Navy Avenger aircraft disappeared while on a training flight from Fort Lauderdale in Florida.

Above: This map shows the area of the so-called Bermuda Triangle in the Atlantic Ocean.

JUNE

25 CENTS
IN CANADA 30 CENTS

AMAZING STORIES

Scientifiction
Stories by

A. Hyatt Verr

John W. Campbe

Edmond Hamil

Left: *Amazing Stories* magazine cover from 1930 pictures a "non-gravitational vortex" in the Atlantic and its effect on ships.

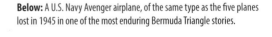

EVIDENCE

THERE IS NO EVIDENCE OF ANY UNNATURAL OR ESPECIALLY DANGEROUS CONDITION AFFECTING THE BERMUDA TRIANGLE. ALLEGATIONS THAT COMPASSES BEHAVE ODDLY THERE ARE NOT TRUE. NOR ARE ROGUE WAVES (WAVES OF UNUSUAL HEIGHT) MORE COMMON THERE THAN ANYWHERE ELSE.

Radio contact was lost and the five planes were never seen again. It is presumed the pilots got lost, ran out of fuel and ditched in heavy seas, too far from their anticipated position for any hope of rescue to reach them in time.

Such ocean tragedies were all too common before modern navigational aids, such as GPS and rapid-response air-sea rescue. Before the 20th century and on-board radio, it was not unusual for a vessel to leave port, head out across the ocean on a regular passage and never be heard of again.

This has not stopped fantastic theories being put forward, however, about the disappearances. These include tales of magnetic anomalies, force-fields, UFO landing sites and undersea cities, such as Atlantis, with power crystals lying on the seabed causing the catastrophes above.

Below: A U.S. Navy Avenger airplane, of the same type as the five planes lost in 1945 in one of the most enduring Bermuda Triangle stories.

Above: *Mary Celeste's* skipper Captain Benjamin Briggs. In a letter to his mother before sailing, he said he hoped to have "a pleasant voyage." In their haste, the crew left clothes and even their pipes behind, but Briggs took the ship's papers.

Below: Rum barrels in a ship's hold. The *Mary Celeste's* crew were unlikely to drink the raw alcohol that constituted their cargo, but fear of an accident may have led to panic.

GHOST SHIP

The *Mary Celeste* is one of the most mysterious ghost ships in the annals of the sea.

On December 5, 1872, the British ship *Dei Gratia* was about 650 km (400 miles) east of the Azores in the North Atlantic. Spying a sailing vessel steering erratically, the *Dei Gratia's* skipper sent a boat to investigate and found the U.S. registered brigantine *Mary Celeste*, with not a soul on board.

The *Mary Celeste*, captained by Benjamin Briggs, left New York on November 7, 1872, with nine people on board. The last log-entry was at 8:00 am on November 25, with an unfinished message from ship's mate Albert Richardson to his wife. There was no other clue as to why the ship had been abandoned; reports that the galley fire was still alight, with still-warm cups of tea on the table were not true. An inquiry at Gibraltar concluded the crew might have got drunk (the ship's cargo was alcohol), killed the Captain, his wife and small child and taken to the ship's boat.

Did the crew mutiny? Did pirates attack the *Mary Celeste*? Or did everyone on board panic, and if so, why? There was no sign of a fire or explosion, but something caused the people to abandon ship. Once in the lifeboat, they would have made for the island of Santa Maria, only 10 km (6 miles) away. However, if a storm had hit suddenly, they would have had little chance in a rough sea on a rocky shore with cliffs.

One possible explanation is that a sailor misread the depth of water in the well of the ship, measured by lowering a sounding rod on a cord down a tube. The *Dei Gratia* sailors noticed the rod lying near its open tube, so "sounding the well" was probably one of the last things the crew did. After its rescue, the *Mary Celeste* continued trading, until wrecked off Haiti in 1885.

Right: A tall ship rigged in the brigantine style, popular for North American ships from the 1700s onwards. The *Mary Celeste* was built to be rigged in the same way, as it made ships fast and easy to maneuver.

Below: This report on the *Mary Celeste* inquiry was published in the New York Times on February 24, 1873.

A Brig's Officers Believed to Have Been Murdered at Sea.

From the Boston Post. Feb. 24.

It is now believed that the fine brig Mary Celeste, of about 236 tons, commanded by Capt. Benjamin Briggs, of Marion, Mass., was seized by pirates in the latter part of November, and that, after murdering the Captain, his wife, child, and officers, the vessel was abandoned near the Western Islands, where the miscreants are supposed to have landed. The brig left New-York on the 17th of November for Genoa, with a cargo of alcohol, and is said to have had a crew consisting mostly of foreigners. The theory now is, that some of the men probably obtained access to the cargo, and were thus stimulated to the desperate deed.

The Mary Celeste was fallen in with by the British brig Dei Gratia, Capt. Morehouse, who left New-York about the middle of November. The hull of the Celeste was found in good condition, and safely towed into Gibraltar, where she has since remained. The confusion in which many things were found on board, (including ladies' apparel, &c.,) led, with other circumstances, to suspicion of wrong and outrage, which has by no means died out. One of the latest letters from Gibraltar received in Boston says: The Vice-Admiralty Court sat yesterday, and will sit again to-morrow. The cargo of the brig has been claimed, and to-morrow the vessel will be claimed.

The general opinion is that there has been foul play on board, as spots of blood on the blade of a sword, in the cabin, and on the rails, with a sharp cut on the wood, indicate force or violence having been used, but how or by whom is the question. Soon after the vessel was picked up, it was considered possible that a collision might have taken place. Had this been the case, and the brig's officers and crew saved, they would have been landed long ere this. We trust that if any of New-England's shipmasters can give any information or hint of strange boats or seamen landing at any of the islands during the past ninety days, that they will see the importance thereof.

THE TRUTH?

POSSIBLY MARY CELESTE WAS ABANDONED WHEN CAPTAIN BRIGGS FEARED A MISHAP. DID HE THINK HIS SHIP WAS SINKING? IT'S CONCEIVABLE THE CREW PANICKED AFTER MISREADING THE LEVEL OF WATER IN THE HULL, CONCLUDING THE VESSEL WAS HOLED. WITH HIS WIFE AND TODDLER DAUGHTER ABOARD, CAPTAIN BRIGGS MAY HAVE LET HIS HEART RULE HIS HEAD AND ABANDONED SHIP, ONLY FOR THE SHIP'S BOAT TO BE OVERWHELMED BY A RISING STORM WHILE THE MARY CELESTE SAILED ON ALONE.

MALAYSIAN FLIGHT MH17

On July 17, 2014, disaster hit another Malaysia Airlines plane. Flight MH17, a scheduled flight from Amsterdam to Kuala Lumpur, Malaysia, was shot down while flying over the border between Russia and Ukraine. It crashed to the ground, killing all 283 passengers and 15 crew on board.

The crash happened during the ongoing civil war between pro-Russian separatist insurgents and Ukrainian forces in eastern Ukraine. The plane appeared to have been brought down by a surface-to-air missile. American and German intelligence sources, and others, were satisfied that the missile had been fired from territory controlled by the pro-Russian rebels. The Russian government, on the other hand, blamed the Ukrainian government for the strike. An investigation is ongoing into the cause of the crash, but what is certain is that the 298 people who died had nothing to do with the conflict.

Above: MH17 was built five years before MH370, but proponents of the theory that the planes were switched say photos show MH17 had the extra window of the newer model. Aviation experts were quick to debunk this theory.

THE TRUTH?

A REPORT IS AWAITED FROM THE OFFICIAL DUTCH INVESTIGATION INTO THE CAUSE OF THE CRASH OF MH17, AND ON THE LIKELY PERPETRATORS OF A SURFACE-TO-AIR MISSILE STRIKE IF THAT WAS THE CAUSE. MANY PEOPLE SAW FLIGHT MH17 TAKE OFF FROM AMSTERDAM EARLIER THAT DAY, AFTER BEING BOARDED BY ITS DOOMED PASSENGERS. THE RELATIVES ALSO RECEIVED THE REMAINS OF THEIR LOVED ONES FOR BURIAL.

Above: Wreckage from MH17 came down in a remote area of eastern Ukraine.

Above: Russian President Vladimir Putin insists the Ukraine government bears full responsibility for the crash because it happened in Ukrainian airspace. He denies the pro-Russian rebels were armed by Russia.

Above: Coffins bearing the remains of people who died in the crash of Malaysia Airlines flight MH17 at a ceremony at Eindhoven Airport in the Netherlands.

Below: Protesters outside the Russian embassy and UN offices in Kuala Lumpur demanded justice for the deaths of the passengers on MH17.

Almost immediately, conspiracy theories began to emerge. Several of the passengers worked on HIV/Aids research and were travelling to a conference. Was the plane shot down by the global elite, the New World Order, who want to depopulate the world and therefore prevent a cure for Aids being revealed? A more popular theory linked MH17 with MH370, also Malaysian Airlines—and said they were actually both the same plane. The 'passengers' were the corpses from MH370, which was landed on Diego Garcia and packed with explosives, allegedly by the CIA. It was then flown over the Russia-Ukraine border where it was blown up to implicate one side in the conflict. Pro-Russian rebels encouraged this story by saying the bodies they found had been dead for many days, and that their passports looked surprisingly new.

MALAYSIAN FLIGHT MH370

On March 8, 2014, Flight MH370 disappeared from the face of the planet. Satellite technology suggested the plane flew for 7 hours off radar and off route. Despite the most expensive search-and-rescue operation in history, no crash site has ever been found.

Flight MH370 left Kuala Lumpur for Beijing with 239 passengers on board. Less than an hour after take-off, air traffic control lost contact. At 7:24 am, the plane was reported missing. Yet 55 minutes later, the satellite Inmarsat picked up an unscheduled 'partial handshake' from the Boeing 777. It was the world's last known contact with Flight MH370.

As Malaysia Airlines released contradictory statements, conspiracy theories thrived. The final voice contact was at 1:19 am: "All right, good night"; the lack of a call sign sparking rumours that the plane may already have been hijacked— perhaps by the two Iranian passengers travelling on stolen passports, or terrorists linked to Al-Qaeda? A minute later, the plane's transponder was switched off.

Inmarsat records indicate that the plane then diverted from its specified route, along either a northern or southern corridor. Had it flown north, as an unidentified airliner entering foreign airspace, and could it possibly have been shot down by fighter jets? Author Nigel Cawthorne attributes the disappearance to a possible U.S. Thai fighter-jet training drill.

THE TRUTH?

THE JOINT AGENCY COORDINATION CENTRE (JACC) BELIEVES THE FINAL, PARTIAL HANDSHAKE FROM FLIGHT MH370 TO INMARSAT CAME FROM THE IMPACT OF IT CRASHING INTO THE INDIAN OCEAN, PROBABLY WHEN ITS FUEL RAN OUT. BUT WHO WAS IN CONTROL OF THE PLANE AT THE TIME, AND WHERE THE PLANE IS NOW, REMAINS A MYSTERY.

Below: Satellite image made available by the AMSA (Australian Maritime Safety Authority) shows a map of the planned search area. Six countries joined the search which resulted in a recovery effort, after authorities announced that the airliner crashed in the Southern Indian Ocean and that there are no survivors.

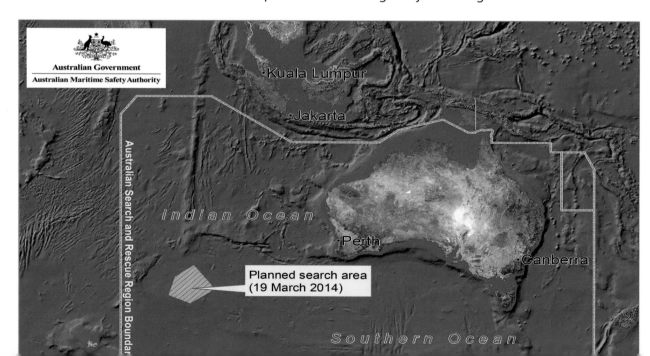

Left: A piece of debris from the missing flight is displayed during a remembrance ceremony on the fifth anniversary of the disappearance.

Below: A Malaysia Airlines flight on approach to land at Melbourne International Airport.

Flight MH370 may also have hidden in the shadow of Singapore Airlines flight 68 (SIA68) to escape detection, before flying on to an unknown destination. Others suggest the plane landed at the remote U.S. air base Diego Garcia (something the Americans have flat-out denied). If the plane flew south, as the authorities believe, it may have hit a "Devil's Graveyard"—an alternative "Bermuda Triangle"—as identified by researcher Ivan Sanderson.

Another theory suggests a plotted and carefully constructed life insurance scam or corporate attack to steal technology that some of the plane's passengers had created (but not yet patented)—every speculation has been considered and investigated. But there are still no answers.

It's possible the plane was doomed from the start. After all, it was the 404th Boeing 777 plane to be produced. As reddit user i-am-SHER-locked put it: "An 'HTTP 404' error means 'not found'. Coincidence? I think not."

Above: Malaysian Prime Minister Najib Abdul Razak updates the media on the search and rescue plan for the missing passengers during a press conference on March 15, 2014 in Kuala Lumpur, Malaysia.

Above: Journalist Mike Sommer displayed radar evidence at a conference looking into conspiracy theories behind the crash.

Below: A photograph from the 1997 hearing investigating the tragedy, and how it occurred.

TWA FLIGHT 800

On July 17, 1996, TWA Flight 800 left New York for Paris. Eleven minutes after take-off it plummeted into the Atlantic Ocean. All 230 people aboard died, but were they victims of a tragic accident, or a missile strike?

In June 2013, a TV documentary re-aired the Flight 800 controversy. Former crash investigators refuted the official verdict, insisting there had been an explosion outside the aircraft, not inside. There were reports that people had seen a missile. Or was it a bomb? According to the authorities, Flight 800 was brought down by internal electrical failure that caused a fire.

TWA Flight 800 left JFK airport in New York for Paris. The aircraft was a Boeing 747, one of the early 1971-series. About 32 km (20 miles) southwest of East Hampton, New York, it was blown apart. Some witnesses (one a Vietnam veteran pilot) claimed to have seen a missile trail. Had Flight 800 been shot down by terrorists? No terrorists claimed responsibility. Three U.S. Navy submarines and a missile-cruiser were in the vicinity. Had a test-fired missile hit the 747 by mistake? Why the media blackout and were the authorities hiding the facts to avoid passenger-panic?

Parallels were drawn with Pan Am Flight 103, blown up by a terrorist bomb over Scotland in 1988. Had Flight 800 been brought down by a bomb? There were allegations that crash investigators found explosive residues under seats in the wreck. The authorities insisted that any explosive traces were left over from routine training exercises with sniffer dogs taught to detect bombs.

THE TRUTH?

AFTER A FOUR-YEAR INVESTIGATION, THE U.S. NATIONAL TRANSPORTATION SAFETY BOARD (NTSB) REJECTED THE MISSILE/ BOMB HYPOTHESIS, DECIDING THAT AN ELECTRICAL SHORT-CIRCUIT IN THE PLANE'S FUEL SYSTEM WIRING STARTED A FIRE THAT IGNITED FULL TANKS OF INFLAMMABLE AVIATION FUEL. THE NTSB ISSUED 15 SAFETY RECOMMENDATIONS TO IMPROVE AIRCRAFT DESIGN. CHARGES OF A COVER-UP REMAINED.

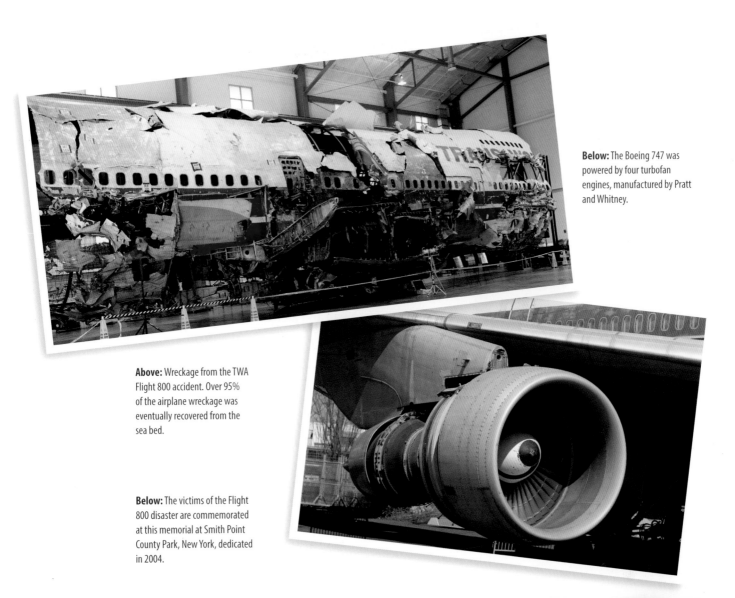

Below: The Boeing 747 was powered by four turbofan engines, manufactured by Pratt and Whitney.

Above: Wreckage from the TWA Flight 800 accident. Over 95% of the airplane wreckage was eventually recovered from the sea bed.

Below: The victims of the Flight 800 disaster are commemorated at this memorial at Smith Point County Park, New York, dedicated in 2004.

THE TWA FLIGHT 800 INTERNATIONAL MEMORIAL

WHAT SANK *TITANIC*?

No ship has spawned more words, pictures, facts and fantasy than *Titanic*, sunk after striking an iceberg in April 1912. The tragedy was real, but is still surrounded by speculation.

Titanic was the largest ship in the world. In April 1912, it was on its first voyage from Southampton to New York, carrying more than 2,000 people. The North Atlantic that season was particularly dangerous because of floating ice farther south than was usual. Titanic received radio warnings of ice, when less than 640 km (400 miles) from New York. Steaming through the night at speed, it hit an iceberg. Ship's lookouts saw the berg when only 500 m (1,640 ft) away and alerted the bridge. First Officer Murdoch took evasive action, steering to port and ordering "stop engines" and "full astern." But it was too late to halt 46,000 tons of luxury liner. *Titanic*'s steering was not up to high-speed maneuvers and as the ship veered, the iceberg sliced along its starboard (right) side, breaching five of 16 watertight compartments. Designer Thomas Andrews knew his ship could not float for long. He and Captain Smith also knew *Titanic* had insufficient lifeboats. The ship sank in just over two hours and over 1,500 people died, among them Andrews and Smith.

Controversy surrounded the action of the ship closest to the stricken liner, the *Californian*. It saw *Titanic*'s lights and distress rockets, but did not steam to the rescue until too late. Conspiracy theories came later, the most unlikely that it was not *Titanic* that sank, but its sister ship *Olympic*, the two ships having "switched identities" after *Olympic* collided with a naval vessel and needed repairs.

Robert Ballard found the wreck of *Titanic* in 1985, more than 3,700 m (12,000 ft) down. The ship lies in two pieces, bow and stern sections having broken apart.

Above: Icebergs are notoriously dangerous because only a small part of the floating iceberg is visible above water, the rest being submerged beneath the surface, a menace to any ship passing too close.

Below: Passengers carried their belongings in trunks and suitcases, each marked with a White Star Line baggage label.

THE TRUTH?

AS SO OFTEN WITH *TITANIC*, SOME CHOOSE TO BELIEVE THE UNLIKELY OVER THE PROBABLE. REPORTS AT THE TIME WERE INEVITABLY CONFUSED. FOR EXAMPLE, THE SHIP'S MUSICIANS WENT ON PLAYING AS THE SHIP FOUNDERED, BUT NO ONE IS 100% SURE WHAT TUNE WAS THEIR LAST, THOUGH IT WAS PROBABLY THE HYMN "NEARER MY GOD TO THEE."

Left: A White Star Line poster advertising the world's largest liner's maiden voyage to America in 1912.

Below: *Titanic* and sister ship *Olympic*. One theory, barely credible, is that the ships were deliberately switched, for insurance and scheduling reasons and that an accident was supposed to be "staged," but went disastrously wrong. *Olympic* steamed on until scrapped in the 1930s.